Sherlock Holmes
and
Dr. John Watson:

A Study in
Illusions of Terror

Sherlock Holmes
and
Dr. John Watson:

A Study in
Illusions of Terror

A novel by
Victor G. Haddox
and
Earl F. Riley

ALMOND
ORCHARD
PUBLICATIONS

Published by

Almond Orchard Publications
6520 PLATT AVE #174
WEST HILLS, CA 91307-3218
AlmondOrchardPub.com
(855) 500-3633

ISBN 13:   978-1-939408-47-1
ISBN 10:   1-939408-47-4

Foreword

Many of our friends and acquaintances have asked the question, "Why did the two of you undertake to write a Sherlock Holmes novel?"

My co-author and colleague, Vic Haddox, answers in something of the following fashion "Holmes is far and away the most popular and widely read fictional detective of all time. He has lasted for nearly a century, and there are no indications that he will not be around for another hundred years. Why shouldn't we try it?"

My partner's answer is a good one, but I think there's more. With Holmes it is always a case of Good vs. Evil. He is squarely on the side of the victim, always holding the shield of truth against the wickedness and depravity of the criminal. To a youth reading his adventures for the first time, he was a hero figure, in the vanguard of the forces of justice. Twenty years later, after having suffered some bruises in the accommodations of modern life, that same youth, now a man, re-reading Dr. Watson 's narratives, more fully appreciates the purity of Holmesian resolve and the clarity of his vision.

I was introduced into the world of Sherlock Holmes in my pre-teens, sometime between Dick and Jane and first year Latin. Every few years since then, I've read again one of the Arthur Conan Doyle tales, and, like the junk food commercial, 'you can't eat (read) just one.'

Then, too, most of us feel we can write a book.

I have no recollection as to how the subject came up, but at a Christmas party in 1979, Vic Haddox and I got to talking about Holmes and Watson. He had a story outline, and he had written a draft of some of the scenes and the accompanying dialogue to flesh out his literary sketch. He was involved with a law practice, a psychiatric practice, some teaching, some real estate development and a host of other business matters, and he was looking for a partner. He gave me his materials, and after many, many sessions with him, his type writer and mine, this is the end result.

Aficionados of Holmesian lore will find certain familiar characters who have appeared in other achievements of his. Mrs. Hudson yet presides over 221 Baker Street, and Billy remains as her page. The head of the Baker Street Irregulars, the ubiquitous Wiggins, is helpful, as is Tobias Gregso from Scotland Yard. Baron Adelbert Gruner is now, as he was then, a villain. Godfrey Staunton and Albert Bray lend their assistance. There is a passing reference to Professor Moriarity and Colonel Sebastian Moran. Near a central figure in any of the Holmes plots, brother Mycroft remains a part, albeit an essential one, of the periphery here.

We have presented some fresh personalities and some new scoundrels. Hopefully, the reader will approve of their inclusion among the Holmes immortals. And, of course, no tale of this 'master of scientific deduction' would be complete without the presence of the pertinacious Inspector Lestrade. He has a prominent role in Illusions of Terror.

The historical scholar will note that at least three new concepts make their initial appearance here. In Book I, a 'psychological profile' of Holmes is introduced. As a psychiatrist, the co-editor of this memoir, Dr. Victor Haddox, advises that his research has uncovered no prior development and use of such against a particular individual, here, Holmes. At the present time, the psychogram, as it is sometimes called, is commonly compiled upon all major political candidates. It is also utilized by law enforcement, based upon a description of the events surrounding the incident, for the unknown perpetrator of a crime. The 'psychological profile' of today's world appears to have been initiated by the criminal genius of this work, but it was Dr. Watson who first realized the dangers presented to the subject.

In Book II, the late 19th century version of the modern photo lineup is employed. Nothing similar appears in prior contemporary literature as an investigative tool of the police establishment.

Lastly, in Book III, the use of steel as a means of protecting individuals is revealed. As a matter of history, Winston Churchill in the first days of World War I counseled its use in the tanks of the British Army for the safety of the personnel of the English armored units in their deployment against the German Army.

In each of these three areas of conduct, Holmes, as usual, was ahead of his time.

With regard to the historical references in this book, the writers have taken, as to dates only, modest literary license. William Gladstone and Herbert Asquith, as Prime Minister and Home Secretary of the English government in the 1890s, were the sponsors of land reform and tax relief legislation for the Irish farmers, and the Gladstone cabinet fell on the issue of Home Rule for Ireland, although the Liberal Party remained committed to that plank in its platform ever after.

If the reader is shocked at the 'hard line' taken by Queen Victoria vis-a-vis her son, Prince Edward, be reminded that the Queen was not that fond of the Prince of Wales. Queen Victoria had lost her beloved husband, Prince Albert, years before, when the Prince Consort had become fatally ill during a journey in which he attempted to mediate one of his son's extramarital affairs. It is doubtful that Prince Edward was ever forgiven, although Victoria's reverence for the traditional succession to the Throne was evident.

The historical facts as to the self-governing status of Canada and Australia, as detailed in Susan's entreaty to Dr. Watson, are true. Her suggestion of a confederation became an actuality at The Imperial Conference of 1926, at which The British Commonwealth of Nations was formally established. This lady, too, was advanced beyond her years.

And, while the verification of all that went on at 55 Eaton Terrace may be questionable, there indeed was such a place. It was a 'house of pleasure,' and some of the royal money may have sustained it.

History does in fact record that Douglas Hyde and Professor Eoin MacNeill founded the Gaelic League, and that John O'Mahoney and his family established the Irish Republican Brotherhood, the forerunner of the Fenians. Herbert Asquith was one of the attorneys for Charles Stewart Parnell at a time before the period encompassed within this book, and the name of Parnell is likely to evoke near genuflections on the part of the Irish cognoscenti.

A very personal expression of gratitude is lovingly extended to our two Sues - Sue Haddox and Sue Canter, our wives. For their unstinting support, we have named the central female character in this book 'Susan.'

Lastly, my Sue on several occasions has commented to our friends about my self-discipline in committing Vic's story to paper. I thank her for the compliment, but it is undeserved. She, for once in her life, has been wrong. It has not been self-discipline; it has truly been a labor of love. Once my routine had been established - of coming home after work in the late afternoon or early evening, and committing myself to one or two hours at the desk or the typewriter - I found myself looking forward to the experience with anticipation.

How many people have had the opportunity and joy of spending, almost daily, some time alone with Sherlock Holmes. It is I who have been enriched by the encounter.

Earl F. Riley

Los Angeles, California

October, 1985

Victor G. Haddox

To the two Susans in our lives -

Susan Haddox

and

Susan Canter –

our wives –

we affectionately dedicate this book.

Prologue

The reticence of my friend, Mr. Sherlock Holmes, to reveal to the world anything of a delicate or scandalous nature has resulted in my deposit of this manuscript with my solicitors, to be made available for publication only upon the demise of all the parties.

I share his reluctance, but for different reasons. It was through this case that I became aware of the dangers presented to my friend, Holmes, by reason of my prior memoirs having appeared in the Strand Magazine. The written accounts of those adventures provided one of the greatest criminal geniuses of all time with a perilously penetrating insight into the personality of my friend, and inadvertently revealed to this evil fiend not only his great strengths, but several of his weaknesses as well.

A full report of the happenings herein requires that I disclose exactly how the knowledge gleaned from my previous publications was turned against Holmes. To rush precipitously into print would, I fear, be an open invitation to similar attempts by lesser, but no less dangerous, heinous malefactors.

Occasional references to isolated incidents in this matter, generally stressing the activities of Inspector Lestrade, have appeared in various newspapers and tabloids over the years. Infrequently, the involvement of my friend has been mentioned, sometimes almost in passing. However, this manuscript presents for the first time a complete narrative of the political intrigue and bizarre danger that surfaced in the highest councils of government, and, while it endured, threatened the Empire itself.

As a further consideration, the premature disclosure of this adventure could well contribute to the political unrest currently festering in the British Isles, a turmoil which I fear may continue for a hundred years and a delay in the publication of this writing may aid the scholar and the historian in placing this period of turbulence into its proper context.

In recounting the exploits of Sherlock Holmes over the decades, my readers have enjoyed a plethora of crime and a myriad of solutions. It is hard to imagine any sort of nefarious activity in which my friend has not been asked to lend his talents on the side of the law and in aid of the unfortunate victims. He had dealt with mysterious disappearances, secret papers, extortion, jewels and treasure, ciphers and conundrums, indiscretions in high places - indeed, the entire gamut of the lawbreaker. Rarely has he become cynical, and to the best of my knowledge, he has never refused a cry for help.

While, on infrequent occasions, he has intervened on request in some matter involving the government, his intellectual stimulations lay in other directions He simply was not interested in affairs of state. I have often remonstrated with him on what I perceived to be a deplorable indifference to the political process and its effect on the lives of his fellow citizens. To all of this, his usual rejoinder was, "Watson, unless and until I am presented with a case in which Whitehall, or one of its public servants, is apparently criminally inculpated, I shall not bother it and I trust that Whitehall will not molest me."

Even after the adventure, which I am now ready to commit to writing, had been brought to a conclusion, he reverted to this posture on events governmental. But for one brief period in his life, Sherlock Holmes became entirely immersed in the happenings of the regency at the very highest levels.

It all began on a warm spring day in May.

Book I:
Of
Mysteries
and
Death

A Graven Tale

As I ascended the steps to our flat at 221B Baker Street, it would have been impossible to have foretold what would confront me upon opening the door. Holmes was kneeling on the floor, staring straight into the muzzle of his pearl handled pistol which was secured by a vise on his workbench about fifteen feet away. A stout cord ran from his finger, around his jackknife stuck in the table, to the weapon's trigger.

His hand pulled the string and the report of the firearm assaulted my eardrums. Holmes was thrown backwards to the floor violently. I dropped the book I was carrying and rushed to my friend. "My God! What have you done?"

Unbelievably, I saw Holmes' corpse sit up, grimacing as his lips pulled away from his teeth. Using his thumb and forefinger, he grasped the ball which was clearly lodged between his teeth. Handing it to me, he said, "Watson, would you hold this for me?"

Rising to his feet, my friend examined the gun, and then turned his attention to a shattered goblet which he had placed directly in the line of fire. He smiled, and said, "An interesting illusion but not nearly as dangerous as RobertHoudin, or his son, Emile, would have one believe."

I sat down, shaking with reaction. I had known of my friend's interest in illusion and prestidigitation, but I had been unaware that he was a practitioner of the more alarming feats of magic. He had employed his sleight of hand talents on several prior occasions to surreptitiously recapture an embarrassing letter or document, and thus to thwart a blackmailer. But, until now, he had never exposed himself to harm by his own hand in any of his experiments in the occult arts.

I picked up the TIMES and pretended an absorption in its contents in order to hide my anger at Holmes for his insensitivity in subjecting me to such an outrageous spectacle without warning. The paper was open to a story regarding the forthcoming London premiere performance of the famous Indian fakir, Ramo Samyi. It contained an account of his triumphant continental tour, and I surmised it to have been the stimulus for my friend's shocking performance.

Ramo Samyi, according to the article, was a man of mystery. Little was known of him except from tales told by occasional mountebanks who had traveled the Indian subcontinent. It was said that his feats could not be duplicated by anyone from the Occident. Several continental magicians had been inspired to imitate his performance and had been injured in the attempts. Two were known to have died. The report also alluded to his guru, who had never left India, but was rumored to be capable of marvels even more astounding than those of his now famous pupil.

My pretense of indifference was for naught, as Holmes had failed to notice my behavior. He had fallen into a brooding silence. It had been several weeks since anything of note had occurred and my friend was not one to take these periods of ennui with casual good nature. His mind thrived on challenge, and when none was present he often turned to study, experiments or drugs to fill the void. Most of the many monographs he had authored had been written during these periods.

The fakirs of India held a special interest for me by reason of my service during the Second Afghan War with the Fifth Northumberland Fusiliers as their Assistant Surgeon.

In my opinion no Occidental illusionist could match the incredible phenomena I had witnessed in India and Afghanistan. The most amazing exploit that I observed was the live entombment of a fakir, which I proceeded to relate to Holmes in an effort to bring him out of his depressive introspection.

"Holmes," I said, "when I was attached to the Fusiliers, and first arrived in Afghanistan, I saw marvels that defy explanation. "

My friend was not one to allow a statement of this nature to remain unchallenged. Indicating by his indulgent smile that he was cognizant of my ploy, Holmes, nevertheless, showed his willingness to respond.

"As you are well aware, Watson, it is an old maxim of mine that when one excludes the impossible, whatever remains, however improbable, must be the truth. Given sufficient facts, nothing cannot be explained."

"I tell you, Holmes, I witnessed the performance of religious rites that defy scientific explanation. I particularly recall one fakir in Qandahar who voluntarily allowed himself to be buried alive for two weeks.

"In my capacity as Assistant Surgeon of the regiment, I examined this holy man. He was emaciated through a period of long training and abstinence. He subsisted only on milk and yogurt. He bathed in steaming hot water, followed by plunges in a cold river. Daily, he sat in a basin of warm water, drawing the wetness up into his intestines and then flushing his bowels. On the day of his burial he swallowed twenty yards of silk ribbon. He then withdrew it, cleansing his entire system of undigested food.

"I inspected his mouth and noted that the base of his tongue had been cut so that it could fall back and block his throat during the burial. He laid down on a length of wood and folded his arms. As I continued my examination, he entered into a state of nirvana and his breathing became imperceptible. His heart stopped. There was absolutely no pulse. He literally died before my eyes.

"His assistant sealed his eyes, ears and nose with wax. The plank was lifted and the holy man was carried to his grave.

"The excavation was well over six feet deep, and at the bottom a wooden vault lined with cloth had been prepared. I was told that this was to protect the fakir from worms and decay during his entombment. After he had been laid to rest, wooden staves were placed over the crypt to shelter his body from the crushing weight of the earth which was rapidly thrown atop his tomb. Blooming flowers were then planted on the surface.

"Two of his disciples seated themselves in the lotus position at the foot and head of the grave, and remained there with minimal sustenance being brought to them by the faithful.

"Two weeks later, I attended the resurrection of this saintly man. An examination of the ground and of the growing flowers demonstrated conclusively that the fakir had not been secretly exhumed, but remained buried in the earth below."

At this point Holmes, who had been silent throughout, quietly interrupted me.

"Watson, assuming that the soil and vegetation were undisturbed, all that would prove is that the man did not exit via the obvious route. There are, however, other possibilities. Pray continue."

"The floral blossoms were carefully picked and distributed to the devoted followers, and the undisturbed dirt was carefully removed. The wooden staves on top of the crypt were lifted, revealing the fakir in the same position as when buried. He was taken from the grave and placed on a prayer rug. The wax plugs that had been inserted in his cranial orifices were carefully removed. He appeared to be dead. He had no pulse, heartbeat or respiration, although there was no sign of decomposition.

"But, astoundingly, within minutes, I saw a slight tremor of his eyelids, and his eyes began to open. His chin fell and his tongue began to flutter. His first breaths were shallow, but soon became deeper and more normal. He began to pray in a weak, almost inaudible voice, which gradually became stronger as he went along, praising God for his survival through divine intervention.

"It was the most singularly inexplicable phenomenon I have ever witnessed in my capacity as a medical doctor."

For a moment Holmes pondered that which I had related, and then asked, "What was the man wearing?"

"He was barefooted, and was dressed in a white loincloth only."

"Did you notice any fecal or urinary staining of the loincloth?"

"No."

"Was it dry and dusty, or was it damp with marks of perspiration?"

"No, it was clean or at least as clean as one usually finds in India."

"Watson, did you notice the man's whiskers, hair and fingernails? Had they grown?"

"I recall that the fakir had been cleanly shaven and his fingernails and toenails had been neatly trimmed in preparation for his burial. When he was exhumed he was still beardless and his nails and hair did not seem to have grown."

"Was his skin bleached from being interred in the ground for two weeks?"

"Now that you mention it, Holmes, I distinctly remember that his face and hands were much darker than the trunk of his body. In removing him from the grave, his dhoti was displaced slightly and I seem to recollect that his skin was much whiter with a clear demarcation at the level of the loincloth."

Again, Holmes was quiet for a moment, and then he began. "If we take the time to logically examine these facts, and to remove ourselves from the illusion the fakir so skillfully wove around the act of his burial, what do they tell us? You, as a medical doctor, are aware that even after death, bodily functions cease at different intervals of time. One's nails and hair will continue to grow for a short period, and yet you did not notice these phenomena on the mullah. Even if he claimed to have willed all anatomical operations to cease, physiologically he would be unable to control the fading of his skin through the absence of exposure to sunlight Furthermore, the darker face and arms would indicate that he had worn a body shirt.

"Thus, he was not always in his grave, despite the facts which would appear to indicate to the contrary. You also noticed that the skin covered by the breechcloth was much lighter than his remaining exposed flesh. Had I been there, Watson, there is no doubt in my mind that I could have exposed the man for the charlatan he was, had I been so inclined."

"How so, Holmes?"

"From your description, Watson, this incident is not

insoluble. There are many possible explanations, although one is most evident. The manifest solution is predicated on the fact that the man had so many assistants. As you know, Watson, many illusions require elaborate preparations and oftentimes demand considerable misdirection. For this, a magician may utilize one or more of staff. You have described the bottom of the grave as containing a crypt prepared with linen and having wooden sides.

"The most elementary resolution, and the one that is readily apparent, is that the vault must have contained a trap door, and the man simply crawled out through a tunnel, returning just prior to his resurrection. The assistants, Watson, above the man's grave were not to keep him in, but rather guards to keep others from digging him out and discovering he was not there. Furthermore, they served as a constant illusional reminder that the man remained in the ground."

I was not surprised at my friend's ability to provide an adequate and logical explanation for what had heretofore appeared to me to be an inexplicable supernatural marvel. Holmes had had a lifelong interest in magic, and although reluctant to reveal the details of how a particular trick or illusion was accomplished, he often applied his powers of deduction to analyze feats of wizardry which were incomprehensible to the average mind. For Holmes, this was merely a mental exercise in observation, deduction and logical thinking. Through the years he had gained a reputation among the cognoscenti and practitioners of the art as being a highly talented amateur performer and an audience even more critical than other magicians.

At this point I made a minor deduction of my own based on the fact that Holmes usually received courtesy tickets from the more prominent artists upon their London premieres, and the fact that the TIMES had been opened to the announcement regarding the Indian magician.

"Holmes, I shall be pleased to accompany you to the debut of Ramo Samyi."

Holmes smiled and responded, "Watson, my friend, despite your adventures in India and Afghanistan, you are not entirely devoid of deductive capabilities."

The Lady and the Tiger

On the night of the performance, it was obvious that Ramo Samyi's reputation had preceded him. His exhibitions in Vienna and Paris had dazzled not only the unsophisticated commoners, but had also drawn the attention and eventual audience of continental royalty. Unlike European magicians, however, it was widely rumored that he was an authentic phenomenon, and could perform true miracles without the use of trickery, illusion or deception. When being interviewed regarding the source of his abilities, his reply was always equivocal, with a veiled reference to years of tutelage under his guru in India.

The success of his London premiere was exemplified by the fact that every seat in the Egyptian Hall Theatre was occupied. Even Prince Edward, the Prince of Wales, and his boisterous entourage were in attendance in the royal box. His Royal Highness was accompanied by two handsome gentlemen, one wearing the glittering decorations of some foreign nation, and three lovely ladies, one of whom was an extraordinarily beautiful redhead.

In addition to the Prince, there were many of the nobility and several prominent magicians of outstanding reputation. There was also the customary assortment of unusual personalities for whom magic has a particular fascination.

In surveying the gallery, I noticed a rather strange fellow with the stature of a giant, who had apparently purchased an entire box for himself, located directly across the theatre from us on the balcony level. Holmes and I had seen this misformed creature occasionally during other first night offerings of outstanding magicians. It was our speculation that the man's propensity for seclusion was due to the fact that, in addition to being extremely large, the poor chap was afflicted with a severe hunchback condition that undoubtedly made him uncomfortable and caused him to be withdrawn in public. He was always formally dressed in top hat, cane and cape, the latter of which he never removed.

As the lights were dimmed, a hush of anticipation enveloped the audience. Ramo Samyi came out onto the stage and deftly weaved an evening of total enchantment which I will long remember. There were many highlights in his repertoire, but the brightest of them all was the finale. An elephant borrowed from the London Zoo was brought on stage and made to disappear before our very eyes.

The beast was ridden by Ramo Samyi's assistant, Guri, a woman of exquisite Indian features, long raven hair, with the noble bearing natural to the uppercast of that country. The magician covered both the rider and the animal with an enormous red silk cloth. The outline of the girl's head and shoulders were clearly visible as was the form of the elephant, and the slight movement of its trunk as it waved to and fro. Ramo Samyi walked twice around the creature, adjusting the cover and murmuring words of incantation. After they had been draped to his satisfaction, he stepped back to the side of the stage, his place being taken by a young Indian lad, who began a slow drum roll, gradually increasing in tempo to a crescendo. Cymbals clashed from the orchestra pit, and Ramo Samyi spun with his arm outstretched, pointing his index finger toward the covered animal. The cloth slowly collapsed to the stage revealing only the silhouette of Guri standing under it alone.

As the audience gasped, the wizard whipped the silk away. The elephant had disappeared!

Before the thunderous applause died down, a large empty cage was lowered to a position approximately five feet above the stage. The boy reappeared, bringing a ladder, and the fakir's beautiful assistant climbed into its interior. The door was bolted shut and secured by a large padlock. To seal it, a small charcoal brazier was produced, and a dipper of molten beeswax was poured into the keyhole of the lock. He then invited the Prince of Wales to impress his signet ring into the still warm wax.

A rope was attached to the corner bar of the cage, and the other end was handed to Prince Edward. He was requested to keep a steady grasp on it to eliminate twisting or swaying. Ramo Samyi quickly draped the cage with the same silk cloth that had been used in the prior illusion.

The Indian drummer boy again beat out a tattoo, and as I the cymbals crashed, the conjurer flung out his arm and pointed his finger at the cage. The audience had been expecting it to vanish, as had the elephant, but, astonishingly, we saw its outline still clearly visible under the cloth. In the dead silence that followed his failure and embarrassment before the Prince, a monstrous roar was heard from under the silk. The Prince dropped the rope he was holding and jumped backwards. Ramo Samyi ripped the covering from the cage revealing an enormous Bengal tiger pacing back and forth, and snarling his anger at being confined.

At this point the audience lost all restraint and general pandemonium erupted. As His Royal Highness walked over to shake Ramo Samyi's hand, the gallery roared its approval. Prince Edward offered congratulations on behalf of himself, and of all of the spectators, for a magnificent production and a splendid evening's entertainment. He also expressed a wish to extend his personal thanks to the lovely young lady who had so competently assisted during the performance. At this point the magician clapped his hands and the Indian boy scurried offstage.

Upon his speedy return, he whispered a message in the ear of his master. Ramo Samyi then explained to the Prince and to the patrons that unfortunately Guri would not be available to accept his complimentary remarks. It appeared that due to a slight mishap, she had been eaten by the tiger.

The Prince smiled good naturedly, as the audience howled with laughter. On that, the curtain descended and the performance ended.

Two Disappearances Explained and a Third Revealed

The following morning as Holmes and I were having our tea and biscuits, I opened the subject of the preceding night's performance.

"I cannot understand how Ramo Samyi caused that elephant to disappear. I could almost touch his flapping ears, and had he broken wind, I have little doubt that we would have been asphyxiated."

A touch of a wry smile appeared on my friend's face as he replied. "Watson, you are continuing to express your odoriferous biological wit, undoubtedly a remnant of your service in Afghanistan."

Despite Holmes' reply, I knew he was not without humor, and that he enjoyed my occasional scatological remarks.

"Holmes, the man is a marvel. I defy you to explain the disappearance of that pendulously ponderous pachyderm."

My friend smiled indulgently and stepped to the window

overlooking the street. "Watson, you sometimes astound me. Pendulously ponderous pachyderm, indeed, and at nine o'clock in the morning." Then, seriously, "The disappearance of the elephant is elementary. It is the illusion of the lady and the tiger that interests me."

"How so, Holmes?"

"The evanescence of the elephant - I, too, can play your game - could be explained by a number of hypotheses: trapdoor, drop curtain, prisms, mirrors and reflecting surfaces. To the trained and discerning eye, one of these was obvious. Had your attention not been misdirected so effectively by the performer's brilliant use of the red silk cloth, you would have seen past the illusion and perceived the reality. Watson, I would give you an explanation but for my obligation to those who so generously invite me to view their performances to the end that they may benefit from critique without fear that I might reveal their secrets."

"If the disappearance of the elephant is so rudimentary, why was the transformation of the lady into the tiger so provocative?"

"Watson, it is not the illusion created by Ramo Samyi that interests me, but rather it is that Samyi excused her failure to appear by the outrageous statement that she had been eaten by the tiger. That comment was inappropriate under the circumstances, and was obviously an attempt by an accomplished illusionist to disguise a mishap."

"What do you mean, mishap?"

"If I am not mistaken, I need not deduce, and you need not speculate regarding the nature of the misadventure. Our magician even now is hurriedly crossing the street on his way to our door. And I must say, rather rudely, for he has just brushed a fellow pedestrian on the walk."

As Holmes completed his statement, there was a pounding

at our outside portal. We heard Mrs. Hudson, our faithful landlady, exclaiming, "Here! What's all this? Where... You can't go up there!"

Footsteps came bounding up the stairs, and before Holmes could reach the threshold, there was another series of sharp raps on the door to our flat. Upon its being opened, there stood the swami with his knuckles raised to strike yet a third sequence. Beads of perspiration were rolling down his forehead and his sideburns, and the droplets were falling onto his collar. Circles of sweat had appeared under the armpits and extended halfway down his side and back. His clothing, still being worn from last evening's performance, was soiled, stained and wrinkled. Gasping in his agitation, he asked, "Mr. Holmes? May I come in? I badly need your help! My wife has disappeared."

My friend exhibited his usual courtesy and solicitude when confronted by distraught and worried clients seeking his counsel. Gesturing toward an empty chair, often occupied by such patrons, Holmes calmly responded.

"You are welcome. Pray be seated."

Turning to me, he continued, "Watson, would you be kind enough to locate my book of news clippings for this past year."

As I turned to search for the requested volume, our guest began to pace the floor, ignoring Holmes' suggestion that he be seated. As he stalked around the room, he began his tale.

First, he introduced himself, stating that he was seeking Holmes' aid because of the disappearance of his wife during the performance of an illusion of magic at the Egyptian Hall Theatre the preceding evening.

"I've already been to Scotland Yard and a police inspector there was totally indifferent to my plight. He said that Guri's disappearance was probably just a domestic dispute and should be resolved amongst ourselves; that it was not a problem for

Scotland Yard."

As he paused for a moment, Holmes, seeking to get to the essentials of the problem, interjected, "Sir, I should advise you first of all that Dr. Watson and I thoroughly enjoyed your presentation last evening. May I again suggest that you sit down and compose yourself. Thank you. Now, pray tell me, what has happened since last night?"

"If you were in the audience you saw my wife. She is my assistant, Mr. Holmes. As you are aware, of the exhibition last evening was flawless, but for her failure to reappear at its conclusion. The substitution of the tiger for my wife was not to be the finale. As the drum roll gave birth to the tiger, exciting the roar from that magnificent beast, my wife should have materialized out of the explosion of smoke to be at my side. Together we were to have accepted the applause of the house.

"My chagrin was twofold. My wife's failure to appear made the illusion incomplete. I will confess to a feeling of relief when I realized I was the only one in the hall, other than Guri and my one assistant, who would be aware that the final act was missing. But that relief was transformed into irritation, knowing that I had lost the opportunity to present her to the Prince. When he requested that I summon her to the stage, and she failed to attend, I became genuinely concerned that perhaps she was injured in some mishap during the transference with the tiger. Hence, my reference to the Bengal as being the cause of her nonappearance had for me an uneasy element of truth."

Reaching for his pipe, my friend responded, "You are incorrect in one minor detail. Last night I was aware that something was amiss with your transformation of the lady into the tiger. At the very end, when the beast materialized, you gave the appearance of being displeased. Throughout the evening's performance you had maintained a totally professional indifference to the success of your illusions. But at what was obviously intended to be the last act of mystery, your emotions betrayed you, and, to the trained observer, were discernible by the higher pitch and slight tremor in your voice as well as the momentary lapse in your professional bearing. You grimaced slightly in your displeasure and glanced in the direction of the smoke twice before, and once during, your conversation with the Prince. It was at that time I concluded your illusion was imperfect, and naturally could not have been completed until your assistant had rematerialized.

"Shortly before your arrival this morning, I was pondering which of several alternative mishaps could have occurred, and I had winnowed it down to two possibilities. Your presence here today seeking my aid as a consulting detective allows me to deduce that there was at least one other individual who was aware that Guri had failed to appear, and, unlike ourselves, knew it was not caused by a mechanical defect. Pray continue."

The magician proceeded as though he had not heard the comments of my friend.

"As soon as I left the stage, I went to our dressing room, and not finding her there, I immediately began a thorough search of the backstage area. When that proved fruitless, I frantically examined the entire theatre. She was nowhere to be found and my agitation increased a hundredfold.

"I was beside myself with worry. Mr. Holmes, I have been in London once before, but my wife is a stranger to Europe. She would never have left the theatre of her own volition. I immediately reported her disappearance to the police, and I spent all of last night and the better part of this morning at Scotland Yard trying to explain the gravity of the matter to Inspector Lestrade."

At the mention of Lestrade's name, my friend raised an eyebrow, indicating that he was entirely cognizant of the frustration that must have been experienced by Mr. Samyi, who continued his narrative.

"Although I explained the facts to the Inspector in the same manner as I have told them to you, that gentlemen had the effrontery to suggest that perhaps my wife had left as the result of some marital dispute or quarrel. When I assured him that such was impossible, he became very condescending. He said that even if Guri had decided to explore this historic city unburdened by the presence of her husband, no harm would befall her as the London police, in the performance of their duties, diligently safeguard all persons walking the streets of London, whether they be citizen or visitor. The man became absolutely insufferable when I pointed out to him that although I was a foreigner from India, even I had heard of the criminal known as Jack the Ripper.

"Mr. Lestrade abruptly terminated the interview and said the Yard would make a routine investigation if she had not returned within two days. He then suggested that if I insisted on taking immediate action, I could consult you, as you are known to take an interest in unusual cases, even though trivial, and occasionally enjoy some measure of success."

Although my friend seemed oblivious to the derogatory innuendo of Lestrade's gratuitous remark, I muttered to myself, "Insufferable ass," and it was not until they both had turned their heads toward me that I appreciated the fact that I had mumbled it aloud. I noted, however, that my observation was not disputed.

The illusionist continued. "I do not know where to turn, Mr. Holmes. In this country I am without family or friend. You must help me." Whereupon this deeply distressed gentleman put his face into his hands and sobbed soundlessly.

My friend's compassion was never more in evidence. He reached forward and placed his hand on Mr. Samyi's shoulder, and said, "Do not despair. I will do everything I can to locate your wife and to solve the mystery of her disappearance. I shall begin immediately, but you must get some rest. How may we contact you?"

Lifting his head from his hands, Ramo Samyi visibly displayed the hope that my friend's words had engendered. He replied, "My London agent has arranged lodgings for me at the Gore Hotel. I don't know how to thank you, Mr. Holmes."

"I suggest you return to your room, said Holmes. "Please do not undertake any investigation on your own, as to do so could prove dangerous, not only to yourself, but to Guri as well."

Thanking Holmes again, Ramo Samyi departed.

Upon the magician' s departure, I handed the news clipping scrapbook to Holmes, resisting an impulse to again criticize his abominable filing system, as to have done so at that moment would have been singularly inappropriate.

Scanning the pages rapidly, Holmes' index finger pounced upon a black headlined two column item.

"Ah hah! I knew it! Note this story on the infamous Throat Crusher of London. Victims one and three were magician's assistants. You will recall, Watson, we were on the Continent engaged in the Mystery of the Werewolf of Bayern when the Crusher began his five weeks of homicides. The terrified public was yet furious at Scotland Yard's failure to have apprehended the fiend when we returned some three weeks after the last killing."

"Yes," I responded," had you been in London at that time I have little doubt that Lestrade would have enjoyed another of his successes, provided he had overcome his natural reluctance to seek your aid."

"This article, Watson, was written after the death of the fifth and last known victim, Thomas Brown, by appointment,

Cabinetmaker to Her Royal Majesty. It lists each of the victims and the dates of their deaths.

"The first, Beverly Caldwell, was an assistant to the famous American artist, Harry Kellar. The second, James Smith, was an elderly man, a guard at the Johnson Importers Warehouse. The third victim was Alexander Herrmann' s assistant, Harold Dornn."

"Alexander Herrmann," I exclaimed. "Was he not the magician who could make a small card rise out of a glass bowl? A delicate wine glass disappear between his fingertips? And was he not famous for making a man vanish from the heart of a burning fire? In point of fact, as I recall, his act included having Herr Dornn, a man of prodigious strength, lift a twenty-stone weight over his head. Then Alexander Herrmann would levitate man and weight about five feet in the air and cause him to revolve slowly over the first few rows of the audience."

"You are absolutely correct, Watson. Your memory is perfect. But to continue. The Crusher's fourth victim was Thomas Brown's daughter, followed five days later, by Thomas Brown himself. I am sure you will remember there was some speculation that Brown had learned the identity of the diabolical killer, and was himself murdered to ensure his silence."

"Do you find any connection between these senseless slaughters, obviously the work of a maniac, and the disappearance of Samyi's wife, Guri?"

Placing his chin on the steeple of his touching fingertips, Holmes replied, "Although I did not wish to cause further upset to Ramo Samyi, I very much fear that his wife may have fallen prey to this monstrous beast. Further, Watson, although his actions are seemingly those of a madman, and have thus led many, including Scotland Yard, to conclude he is a lunatic, I am not convinced that this man is without reason. Although no one has formally invited me to participate in the investigation of this matter, some deductions should be apparent to anyone who reads the London TIMES and is able to assimilate information."

Holmes thumbed forward in his scrapbook and drew my attention to yet another article. It was a brief item, reporting that two crates containing the esoteric new explosive, dynamite, had been stolen under mysterious circumstances from the Johnson Importers Warehouse. The paper went on to state that the substance, due to its hazardous properties, had been securely secreted within a specially built brick room, entry to which was through a heavy metal door equipped with an exceptionally strong lock. The thief had done no other damage and had left no clues. Inspector Lestrade had arrested several warehouse employees involved in the initial delivery and its security.

Without comment, Holmes handed me yet a third clipping from the following day's edition. It announced that the body of a guard, James Smith, had been found in a carton at the warehouse some eight hours after the discovery of the theft of the dynamite. The report recounted what was known of the loss of the explosive, and drew the rather obvious conclusion that Smith had met his death when in making his rounds he had come upon the thief. His throat had been crushed and his neck broken. The headline on the article read:

DOES CRUSHER NOW HOLD DYNAMITE?

"Watson, I fear we may be pursuing an individual who might well be the most dangerous man in all of Great Britain. He is totally ruthless, and he is using a knowledge of illusion and deception for evil purposes. This is no ordinary criminal, and the Crown itself may be in grave danger."

A Three Pipe Problem

"What do you make of it, Holmes? Do you have any hypotheses? What should we do?"

"Watson, the implications of this case are frightening. I am convinced that this young lady, Guri, is in mortal danger, but it would be premature for me to take immediate action until I have had a chance to think the matter through." Whereupon my friend looked at me, and smiling slightly, said, "And Watson, this is at least a three-pipe problem. "

After making this announcement my friend went to the mantel and filled his calabash from the Persian slipper. Soon, the air around him became as opaque as a London fog and the stench of his odoriferous shag drove me from the room.

I walked the streets of the neighborhood pondering the problem in my own way. Upon my return to our lodgings nearly two hours later, I found that the smoke had won its battle with the oxygen. Holmes sat immobile as though paralyzed by its toxic effects. I did not have to note the two dottles of ashes on the fireplace grate to know that he was on his third pipe. Throughout my long association with Holmes, I had seen him reach this peak of intense concentration only rarely. His pupils were wide and fixed. As I walked in front of him, his eyes did not move but continued to stare through the wall, and I knew he was receptive to no outside stimuli. Instead of the long deep inhalations with which he had initiated his smoking, his breathing was rapid and shallow, and frequent short puffs were exhaled. The skin of his face and hands was reddened and I noticed small beads of perspiration trickling from his hairline. The jugular vein in his neck pulsed rapidly.

For a brief moment I stood in awe of the monumental genius which I knew was grappling with every nuance, every fact and every aspect of the conundrum with which he was confronted. As a jeweler examining an uncut diamond, turning the stone, inspecting its facets, searching for its fracture lines, Holmes sat and struggled with his problem. His concentration was so intense that there was a fine tremor in his fingers as his hands grasped his pipe.

I walked to the window to throw it open. Although, ordinarily, I would have catered to my friend's idiosyncrasy and left it closed, I knew the depth of his engrossment was such as to preclude his notice.

After taking several deep breaths, I turned from the window, and was surprised to see Holmes standing and preparing to leave. As he donned his mackintosh and deerstalker, he said, "Watson, I have accomplished all that I can within the confines of this room. It is time that we investigate in person."

We walked a short distance down Baker Street and engaged a cab at Tussaud's, directing the driver to the Egyptian Hall Theatre. I noted that Holmes had undergone a marked transformation in attitude and personality. He was relaxed and apparently content to enjoy the short ride.

Turning to my friend, I said, "After your assault upon the breathable air has made our flat vaguely reminiscent of the calamity I feared would befall us from our close association with the elephant last evening, I hope that the insights you gained were worth it. What do you make of it, Holmes?"

"As you know, Watson, I have always been reluctant to reveal my theories at the outset of any case. Although I have never taken the time to articulate them, there are many reasons for my not immediately taking you into my confidence. First, oftentimes you serve as my investigator and liaison. I depend on you to report your thoughts and observations. It is necessary that those impressions and facts of yours be uncontaminated by any preconceived theories and interpretations that you may have acquired from me. Secondly, an illusion is sometimes created by the perpetrator of a given crime, and my mind, unlike most others, often cuts through the misdirection, and thus does not perceive the event as expected. It is important to me, therefore, to have an associate who is an accurate observer, but who does not necessarily see through the misleading appearance. Third, it often happens that we are together when I confront witnesses and criminals. During these confrontations, it is important to me that no one, not even yourself, suspect the motives for any of my actions. For example, you know that I am not a clumsy person. Yet, on occasion, I have appeared to be maladroit in order to create a diversion, or to develop an opportunity to examine an object closely without others being aware of my interest. In such a case, Watson, it is I who wish to create an illusion. If you were aware of my purpose, your reaction or lack of it would disclose to one and all my reasoning and intention."

A Dangerous List

After alighting from our cab at the Egyptian Hall, we strolled down, the short alley to the stage door entry. As I reached to ring the bell, Holmes arrested my arm.

"Hullo, what's this!" he exclaimed. He extracted his magnifying glass from his coat pocket and examined the door lock with minute care. Straightening up, he handed the glass to me, saying, "Have a look, Watson; someone has been at this lock with a set of picks, and quite recently, too."

Under the magnifying power of his lens I could make out small nicks and scratches on and next to the keyhole. Some had oxidized with the passage of time, but some were quite obviously new. I was again struck with the acute powers of observation of my friend. He had seen without visual assistance, markings on a metal lock and keyhole, which I was able to visualize only with magnification, and then after they had been pointed out to me. After replacing his glass in its velvet lined case and restoring it to his pocket, Holmes rang the stage door entry bell.

The ring was soon answered by the kindly old guard, George Whitworth, to whom Holmes had rendered some slight assistance several years before.

"Why, Mr. Holmes, and Dr. Watson, too. What would you gentlemen be wishing at this time of day? The theatre does not open its doors until seven, and the performers have not yet arrived."

"As you may know, Mr. Whitworth, Ramo Samyi's wife has disappeared, and we would like to take a look around."

"Certainly, sir," said the guard, opening the door still wider so that we might enter. "I'll turn up some lights for you."

"Half a moment, Mr. Whitworth. There are two questions I would put to you. First, is there a guard on duty all night here at the theatre?"

"Why, no, Mr. Holmes," the custodian replied. "You see, there's two of us. I come down about seven in the morning. I admit the janitors, admit the performers for rehearsals, the stagehands and those. Billings gets here about half after four in the afternoon. We have tea together before I leave. He stays until everybody's gone home, everything's locked up, and the lights are out."

"Thank you, Mr. Whitworth. My second question is this: Has anything been stolen from the theatre within the past three days to your knowledge?"

"Oh, no, sir," he responded "Everything's just as it should be when I go on in the mornings, and has been for three or four years now. Somebody made off with some costumes once - but that's been three or four years like I said."

"Thank you, Mr. Whitworth, and now if we may have some lights, if you please."

"Right away, sir."

At this point my friend strode purposefully past the guard's desk and into the theatre's backstage in the direction of the proscenium. Momentarily, I lost sight of him as my eyes could not rapidly accommodate to the abrupt change from the bright sun of the afternoon to the darkness and shadows of the backstage. Rather than blunder into some obstruction, I paused momentarily until Mr. Whitworth brought up the house lights. I then wove my way through various props and backboards until I came upon the figure of my friend standing center stage before the prompter slowly turning his head from left to right, surveying the entire seating arrangement. As I approached, he turned to me and said, "Watson, I'm going to examine the loges."

As Holmes had not specifically invited me to accompany him, I remained on the stage as I was well aware of his preference for solitude while making an intensive investigation. Furthermore, I did not want inadvertently to disturb any of the areas being studied. I knew my friend to be much too courteous to ask me to remain behind, but our friendship was such that no such request need be made.

Shortly, I saw him enter the lower loge nearest stage left. I was not surprised, even though I knew those had been the seats he and I had occupied the preceding evening. Holmes was not one to assume that just because this had been our box, it would contain no clues. My friend made only deductions based on fact.

Realizing that he intended to make a meticulous search of each and every stall, and that this would take some period of time, my thoughts turned to the performance we had witnessed the night before, and to my 'pendulously ponderous pachyderm.' How had that animal been made to disappear?

Employing my friend's methods, I examined the floor of the stage, and while I found several trapdoors, none approached the size required to accommodate the girth of an elephant.

Not content that I had fully eliminated the use of some means of removing the beast through the floor, I decided to examine beneath the stage in the hopes of finding some devilish mechanism that would account for the disappearance of that colossus. I retraced my steps to the stage door and asked Mr. Whitworth if he would be kind enough to direct me to the basement. He led me to the stairs, and handed me a lantern because the gas jets below were not in use.

Upon my descent, I unexpectedly learned that the sub-stage was fully as large as the one upstairs. I could not imagine the use of many of the devices I observed. None of them, however, appeared to be of sufficient size or strength to lower an elephant. I studied several of the contrivances, but the most interesting one, and the one which most aroused my curiosity, was an apparatus with a complicated hydraulic system, many gears of different sizes, various levers and a number of taut wires. Sitting on the piston of this machine was the cage in which I had last seen Guri just before she had been transformed into a tiger.

As I walked about this amazing instrument, the rays from my lantern highlighted a small, white, folded paper object on the floor. I picked it up, and found that it was last night's programme. Inscribed on the back, and written in a small neat script, I read a column of notations, reciting as follows:

ATHLETICS

Boxer - Expert
Marksman - Expert
Single-stick player - Expert
Swordsman - Expert

FEMME

Naiveté

LAW

Practical Knowledge of Crimes

LITERATURE

Classic - Nil
Modern - Nil
Sensational - Profound

PHILOSOPHY

Nil

POLITICS

Apolitical

SCIENCES

Anatomy -	Only as it relates to crimes
Apothecary -	Profound as to poisons; General - weak
Botany -	Immense as to identification of species, locale and poisons
Chemistry -	Profound
Geology -	Profound but limited to identification of locales

In contemplating this list, my stomach turned sour and my head became light. This tabulation could only be one thing: a very detailed and accurate description of my friend, Sherlock Holmes. But Holmes was a recluse, and who but I knew him well enough to make such an inventory, or to recognize such an enumeration for what it so obviously was? Suddenly, the recognition flooded in upon me that innumerable people could have compiled such a table, and could have acquired the necessary information merely for the price of a few Strand magazines. I had betrayed my friend for some paltry pieces of silver, and in so doing I had revealed his strengths and weaknesses to the world.

I immediately knew that I must bring this list to his attention, but my obligation to do so conflicted mightily with my embarrassment and reluctance to reveal what I conceived to be an unintended and unconscious expose.

I hurriedly returned to the stage. I noted that Holmes had completed the semi-circle of lower boxes, and was now inspecting the loge immediately across from the one we had occupied, and which had been filled last evening by the grotesque giant. Standing just behind the footlights, I called," Holmes, come down and look at this programme. Someone has made some notations on it which I am afraid can only be a description of you."

Holding his magnifying glass near one of the chairs, my friend turned his head, and responded, "I shall be down in a moment, Watson, but first I must finish my examination of this loge. It possesses many contradictions."

I waited impatiently for several minutes, and eventually Holmes joined me on the stage. He examined the writing, and a wry smile came to his face.

"Watson, you have ruined me."

I was crushed. My worst fears had been realized. My

anguish must have been reflected in my expression, because my friend promptly placed his arm around my shoulder and said, "Watson, I believe that you, more than anyone, will be surprised to learn that this list is far from being an accurate description of me. I long ago concluded that your chronicles could make me vulnerable to just this type of analysis. Thus, I have subtly encouraged certain of your wrong impressions regarding my knowledge and personality, and have, in fact, actively encouraged some of those misconceptions. Furthermore, where I felt that your assessments of my weaknesses were accurate, I have surreptitiously bolstered my knowledge and developed my individuality accordingly.

"Be sure, Watson, that this inventory is not nearly as threatening or dangerous as it appears. It is far from accurate. It is ominous, however, in that it conclusively demonstrates that there exists a criminal sufficiently intelligent to have prepared such a study based upon your descriptions of me as printed in the Strand."

"Holmes, do you think it's Moriarity?"

"No, Watson - not Moriarity. The script is minute and does not have the bold slashing style of Moriarity's writing."

"The Crown Jewels are Stolen"

Abruptly, we were interrupted by a loud braying voice from the well of the theatre.

"Ah-hah, the soliloquy from Hamlet, no doubt."

I peered into the pit and made out the silhouette of a rather slightly built man in an overcoat. The clothing and manner of speech could belong only to one person, Inspector Lestrade. Looking down at him and holding my cupped hand forward, the fingers spread toward his neck, I rejoined, "Alas, Lestrade. Here, no doubt, to play the part of poor Yorick."

"Enough of this play acting," said Lestrade. "Your efforts to be in the limelight are becoming ludicrous. Mr. Holmes, I must request that you accompany me at once to the Tower of London. The Towers have been bombed and the Crown Jewels are stolen."

Although I was most upset at the news that the Crown Jewels had been abducted, I was also disappointed. I had leaped to the supposition that Lestrade had had a change of heart, and had decided to assist us in the investigation of the missing Guri.

"How did you find us, Lestrade?" I asked.

"I have my methods, Dr. Watson. I have my methods."

"Yes, I imagine you have," said Holmes. "I told Mrs. Hudson of our destination when we left our flat."

"Your methods! Humph," I muttered.

"Lestrade, compose yourself. How long ago did this attack occur?"

"About half an hour ago, Mr. Holmes. I have instructed my men not to disturb anything until I have returned with you."

"In that case, Lestrade, I shall conclude my investigation here and then accompany you to the Tower. I have learned all I can from my examination of the loges, and it should take less than an hour to inspect the understage and the environs behind the curtain."

"Holmes! One explosion breached the wall of White Tower! During the fire and confusion, several political prisoners escaped from the former banquet room. My preliminary investigation has revealed that most of them are Fenians, the Irish Secessionists whose anarchistic activities are a threat to our civilized form of government, and even to the Royal Family itself. What can possibly be more important than that?"

"If my suspicions are correct," Holmes retorted sharply, "a woman's life may well depend upon the results of the present inquiry. The situation at the Tower will remain stable pending our arrival, due to your foresight in instructing the guards to disturb nothing."

"Yes," I injected, "Lestrade has finally learned a more intelligent investigative approach from observing your methods."

Ignoring my comment, Lestrade continued; "Is this that silly affair involving the magician Samyi and his assistant? That is nothing more than a lover's quarrel, and most certainly not of the magnitude of the explosion at the Tower and the escapees."

"My time could be better spent investigating than in arguing a moot point," said Holmes, turning on his heel and striding purposefully toward the exit on stage left. The argument appearing to have resolved unilaterally, Lestrade and I followed him off the stage.

Just as we reached the stage door, Holmes stopped suddenly.

"Watson, the thought occurs to me that the folded programme with. the notes should not be dismissed lightly. If it were dropped by accident, the party may wish to retrieve it so that it not fall into my hands or into the hands of Scotland Yard. It is equally possible that it was deliberately placed on the floor with the intent that it should be found."

"What would be the significance of someone wanting it found, pray tell?" I asked.

"It may well be that someone wants me to know in an indirect fashion that they are aware that I am on the case," was his reply. "Either way, it might be a wiser course of action on our part to ask you to return the programme to the precise point from which it was taken, and, after concealing your person, keep it under observation to see if someone comes to retrieve it. After Lestrade and I have finished at the Tower, I shall return and continue the investigation."

With that, he was gone. I again descended to the substage and replaced the note on the floor, next to the cage standing upon the piston. In doing so, I noted that my only source of illumination was the lantern I was carrying. If I extinguished it, the whole place would be pitch-black. Assuming I heard someone come for the note, I would be unable to see or identify him. Even if the party brought his own lamp, its beam would undoubtedly be directed in such a fashion that all I might be able to see would be his boots, and though I would make every effort to study them thoroughly, I must admit that I do not possess the powers of observation of detail, from which Holmes can make his uncanny deductions.

After considering several alternatives, I endeavored to solve the illumination problem by lighting a single gas jet located in the wall at the entry to the basement. Since the cage and note were at least forty feet removed from the light, I felt that anyone entering would assume that its purpose was for the safety of a person descending from backstage. I found a spot behind some crates in the corner where I could hide, from which a view of both the entry and the note could be had, and that is where I took my post together with my now extinguished lantern.

Although my temporary quarters were not uncomfortable, with nothing to do except keep one eye on the flickering gas fixture and the other on the note, the wait seemed endless. The silence was absolute. I could hear nothing of the outside world. On one occasion, some boards overhead creaked softly. I assumed it to be Mr. Whitworth making his rounds. I was even grateful for that, for it told me that there was at least one other human being on the periphery of my current existence. I lost all awareness of time, but somewhat later, there was a faint muffled concussive sound, accompanied by a slight tremor in the building. I was curious about the incident, but dared not leave my place of concealment.

Suddenly, the meager light from the gas fixture flickered and died! The darkness was absolute. I strained my eyes trying to penetrate the Stygian blackness. Nothing! I inhaled soundlessly and cautiously to see if whatever or whoever was in that room had any distinctive odor or scent. Nothing! I listened with all my acoustical powers acutely sensitive. I imagined that I heard a series of the faintest of movements, putting one in mind of one piece of cloth being rubbed against another, and barely audible for just a few seconds, and again the utter silence in the darkness. Moments later, there was a gleam of light from the stairway leading to backstage. I could not see the flame itself, but it was undoubtedly another gas jet in the wall, farther up the stairs My line of vision did not permit me to see who had struck the light.

Instinct told me that the occasion for which I had concealed myself had passed and would not return. I bounded out of my observation post to give speedy pursuit in hopes of catching a glimpse of the intruder. As I passed the cage, I saw the note still on the floor. I snatched it up, putting it in my pocket as I raced up the steps, heading for the stage door entry. Perhaps Mr. Whitworth had seen our stealthy visitor.

As I burst out of the passageway just before the stage door, I tripped over something large and soft on the floor, and fell headlong, banging the top of my skull against the door frame. As I sat up, shaking my head to clear my senses, the two things I saw again brought forcefully to my attention the fact that my friend and I were involved in a matter, the depths of which were as yet far beyond us. First, the massive iron bound wooden stage door was on its lock side, with the flange of the hinge against the doorjamb, ripped from its moorings by some unimaginable force. Second, lying some ten or fifteen feet away was the object over which I had tripped and fallen, the body of Mr. Whitworth. He was sprawled partially on his left side, his right leg thrust forward. His head was bent anteriorly at an absurd angle and was almost beneath his chest. It was at once apparent to me that his neck had been broken, but the physician in me asserted itself, and I scrambled over to him to learn if there was any sign of life. Alas, there was none. There were enormous welts on the right side of his face, and his entire cervical spine was vividly discolored. Blood was still seeping from the ruptures of his skin. Even in my years as a surgeon in Her Majesty's service in India, I had never seen such severe traumatic injury to the neck of a human being.

Our Fist Answer

As I climbed to my feet, numbly wondering what Holmes would do if he were here, a carriage pulled up to the stage door entry, and Lestrade and my friend alighted. Seeing my agitation, Holmes quickened his pace, and with long strides entered about four steps ahead of the Scotland Yard inspector. His quick eyes took in everything in an instant, and then he, too, knelt beside the body of the guard. I heard Lestrade's sharp intake of breath before he spoke.

"Here, here, what's going on? Watson's got blood on his hands and the knees of his trousers! By God, he's done the blighter in!"

"Lestrade," Holmes said sharply. "Sometimes you really are a blithering ass. Observe those marks upon the throat. Strangulation - and by the extremely large hands of a very powerful man. None of the three of us could possibly have inflicted those injuries. I daresay none of us know anyone with this kind of brute strength. Furthermore, to suspect Watson of this kind of barbarity, or even think of it, is ludicrous in the extreme."

"You're right, Mr. Holmes. My apology, Doctor," Lestrade mumbled.

Standing up, my friend asked me to recount precisely what had occurred from the time he and Lestrade had left for the Tower of London until the present. I responded in much the same fashion as I have set forth on these pages. After further inquiry about other sounds I might have heard, any draughts I had felt, or anything that might have intruded upon my subconscious, Holmes asked to be taken to the substage so that he might see its physical properties. I showed him the gas fixture I had lit on the stairs, where I had hidden, and where the programme had been on the floor.

"The note, Watson, where is the note?"

I took it from my pocket and handed it to him, explaining that in my pursuit of the person who had ascended the stairs, I had snatched it up and stuffed it in my pocket. He took the folded paper from me, and examined it carefully. Without a word he extended it to me I stared at a totally blank piece of white foolscap and my hand began to shake slightly. "My God, Holmes, what does it mean?"

"It means, my dear Watson," he replied, "that the first note was intended to be found by either you or me, since someone knew we were investigating Guri's disappearance from the stage above us. It was left here to tell us that they anticipated that we would find it in our search, and, finding it, would establish our own surveillance of it. It was taken to show us they could do it under our very noses. And, this," he continued, holding up the blank piece of paper, "was substituted for the original to tell us that they know that we know that they have taken the girl."

"How so, Holmes?"

"Elementary, Watson, just as within the last hour, the first note was removed under our very noses, and this blank paper substituted; in this very theatre, within the last twenty-four hours, the girl was removed from under our eyes and noses, and the tiger was substituted.

"Quickly, Watson, where is the lamp you obtained from Mr. Whitworth when you came down here while I was gone?"

Speedily, I obtained the lantern from my hiding place in the corner. After it was lighted, my friend placed it on the floor near the spot where the paper had been found. Then, on his hands and knees, he began a systematic and thorough perusal of the wood planking and the variously sized rugs and remnants of carpeting, which were scattered about in no apparent design.

With the use of his magnifying glass, he would move backwards and forwards, studying an approximate half circle ahead of the beam of his lamp. When one area of search was completed, he would move his light about four feet to the right or left, as his then pattern of examination dictated, and repeat the process. It was soon apparent that his primary interests were, first, an imaginary path about eight feet wide between his starting point and the bottom of the stairs; and a second area between the piston-borne cage and a seemingly doorless wooden crate, about the same size as the cage, which was standing on a cart about twenty feet away and against the wall. When my friend had completed his methodical scrutiny of the floor area around the undercarriage of the cart, he rose to his feet muttering something about needing my ministrations for his back later.

He then proceeded to give the cage-sized box the same detailed study he had just completed on the floor surface. At his request I located and lit the immediately adjacent gas fixtures to provide greater illumination for his inspection. The two sides and two ends failed to turn up any doors or panels for access. Yet, when he rapped sharply on its exterior walls with his knuckles, we knew it was unmistakably empty. With my assistance he turned it on its side and met with the same results. Again we righted what I confess I had begun to regard as a wooden burial vault. Giving me the lantern to hold for a moment, Holmes climbed up on the cart to examine the carton's upper surface.

"Aha," he exclaimed. "Again, Watson, we have eliminated all other possibilities. Access is, in fact, through the top. There is a sliding panel here which has a travel range of about three feet. It fits quite snugly, and if it had been tightly closed, it might well have been overlooked in a superficial examination. But, for some reason it was left open about four inches." He again slid the panel back, and it was a tribute to a fine cabinetmaker's artistry that the motion did not bind and was virtually soundless.

"Its contents, Holmes, what are its contents?" I asked.

My friend's head and shoulders disappeared from view along with the rays from his lantern as again he bent to his glass-aided study of the interior of the box. At last he straightened.

"Nothing, Watson, absolutely nothing. Not even dust." He closed the box. "And that in itself is interesting, because a very light powder of it coats the upper surface."

So saying, he stared down into its interior for a measurable period of time. Suddenly, he handed the lamp to me, and plunged his head and shoulders far down inside the box, remaining in that position for nearly forty-five seconds. Just as I was about to inquire if he was all right, he emerged slowly into an upright position. He reached out his right hand which I clasped to assist him on his climb down. I noticed he seemed slightly unsteady on his feet, which I mentally diagnosed as a diminution of oxygen to his head and brain, altered dramatically while his head had been thrust deeply into such a confined space. Sure enough, by the time I had noted all this in the medical chart on my friend, which I had kept in my mind for these many years, the momentary loss of balance which he had seemingly experienced had disappeared.

Very thoughtfully, he looked again at the carefully crafted crate, and then turned his attention to the cage in the center of the room, and to the mechanism upon which it was standing. After studying it from all angles, he began to attempt its operation, using the cranks and gears attached. After some minutes of trial and error, and to my utter astonishment and admiration, he became fairly proficient in moving the piston up and down, from side to side, and in a complete circle. Finally, he stepped back, and making the motions of a man dusting his hands, he turned to me.

"Watson, we have acquired some answers. We now know how Guri was abducted. It's chloroform, Watson. The interior of that casket-sized box has a faint odor of chloroform. But there's nothing here to tell us why, the identity of her captors, or where she is.

"Let's go home. Lestrade and his Yard boys can finish the problems of the backstage."

The Queen's Burden

About noon of the second day following the killing of the guard at the theatre, we had a visitor; or, rather, a messenger. The caller was the Queen's nephew, Lord Victor. He brought a handwritten note from Her Majesty inviting Holmes and me to a personal audience at Buckingham Palace at four o'clock. Lord Victor was extremely uncommunicative about it all, saying simply that the Queen's transport would call for us at half past three.

Promptly at the stated hour, a richly appointed four wheeled carriage, drawn by two beautifully matched bays, drew up in front of 221B Baker Street. A uniformed footman alighted and rang the bell. Within moments we were escorted down the stairs, assisted into our conveyance, and we were off to the palace. Upon our arrival, we were shown into the Queen's Chambers. There to my surprise we found not only Her Majesty, but Mr. William Gladstone, the Prime Minister, and Mr. Herbert Asquith, the Home Secretary, as well. This was indeed a heady moment, but it also foretold that this was far more serious than at least I had anticipated.

Once the amenities were concluded, we were seated in upholstered chairs in a semi-circle before the Queen.

"Mr. Holmes, Dr. Watson," said Her Majesty," first of all, permit me to express my deep appreciation for your attendance this afternoon. For many years I have had an abiding interest in your accomplishments, Mr. Holmes, in your services to the people of England, and to some of the royal families of Europe. I am also very much aware, Mr. Holmes, in many of your more notable successes, you have had the assistance and counsel of your friend and companion this afternoon, Dr. Watson. It is because of this, and for reasons of which you shall soon be made aware, Dr. Watson, you, too, are most welcome. Now, with those preliminaries out of the way, I should like to ask the Prime Minister to tell you exactly why it is that you have been summoned here on such short notice. Mr. Gladstone, please."

William Gladstone inclined his head gravely in the Queen's direction and stood up slowly. He stepped behind his chair, and placing his hands lightly upon its back, he began to speak in his distinctive melodious baritone with which he had been able to command respect in the House of Commons for these many years. Indeed, his qualities of leadership had brought him three times to his present exalted post.

"Your Majesty, Home Secretary, Mr. Holmes, Dr. Watson," he began, "You are, of course, aware that two days ago there were two bombings at the Tower of London. The first was in Wakefield Tower, which as you know is where the Crown Jewels were displayed. In that explosion, the collection housed in the central exhibit cabinet disappeared, although the rest of the treasure housed in the cases in the room's corners are intact. The second, about ten minutes following the first, was at White Tower, which is the government's detention for prisoners who had plotted or conspired against the Crown.

Some seventeen felons escaped, the great majority of them Fenians. We assumed at the time that these two incidents of terror were related.

"The events of today have proved our supposition to be correct, which brings me to the explanation for which this meeting was called. Her Majesty received in this morning's post a message which makes certain demands upon the government, and, in addition, contains some most distressing news. I should like to read it to both of you."

The Prime Minister stepped to his left and picked up an unsealed manila envelope from a marble coffee table located to the right of the Queen. Opening it, he extracted two sheets of heavy white paper, which I could see were covered with large block printing. Adjusting his spectacles, the Prime Minister began to read.

"Her Majesty of England, but not of Ireland -

"The Fenians have your son, your so-called Prince of Wales. We are holding him in ransom for the indignities to which your government has subjected the Irish Free Nation for centuries. Your subjugation and exploitation of our peoples must cease, and we are prepared to shed our blood and yours to this end.

"We will trade your son for the remainder of the Crown Jewels and £500,000 in £1 and £5 notes. Our mutual emissary will be Dr. John Watson, the friend of Mr. Sherlock Holmes.

"You are to prepare the jewels and bills in waterproof, buoyant, shock and salt resistant containers for delivery, such preparations to be completed within 24 hours. Sometime after today, Dr. Watson will receive instructions as to the place and means of delivery and exchange.

"We will permit no interference by Scotland Yard, and we are prepared to kill your son and Dr. Watson if there is any undertaking to thwart our plans. Their blood will be on your hands.

"IRELAND FOREVER

"The Fenians"

When the Prime Minister ceased reading, there was a silence lasting several seconds, which was broken by the sound of a hoarse, low voice, saying repeatedly, "What, what, what?" Suddenly, I noticed the heads of those present turning slowly in my direction, and I came stumblingly to the awareness that that croaking vocalization had been my own, expressing my disbelief of all that I had heard and of my proposed part in it.

Holmes was the first in the room to break a silence of several moments which followed Mr. Gladstone's reading of that extraordinary letter.

"First of all, how many people know about this demand?" he inquired.

"As yet, only the five of us in this room, Mr. Holmes," the Prime Minister replied.

"We have not advised Scotland Yard, Mr. Holmes," volunteered the Home Secretary. "We felt it would be preferable to confer with you before we do anything further."

"Has no one talked to the Prince's coachmen or footmen? Surely, they would have some information of value."

"The Royal Chamberlain advises me that his coach and his personal attendants have not been seen for over three days," responded Her Majesty.

"We appreciate the fact that you have just now been made aware of the contents of this message, Mr. Holmes, but are you able to draw any initial conclusions?"

"As yet, I have only questions, Mr. Secretary," my friend responded. "Can anyone tell me when and where the Prince was last seen?"

"As we have said, no one knows about this note and we have therefore made no inquiries, discreet or otherwise," said the Home Secretary, "but we do know that he attended the Ramo Samyi performance at the Egyptian Hall Theatre three nights ago. With him at the time were Godfrey Staunton, the rugby international, a nephew of Lord Mount-James, Baron Adelbert Gruner, and three young ladies of whom the identity is known of but one, Lady Patricia Anne, the daughter of the Duke of Kent. As I say, we have not been in touch with any of them."

"Baron Adelbert Gruner," said Holmes musingly, "why am I reacting to that name?"

To this question, Queen Victoria responded with more than a smattering of asperity.

"A rotter! An absolute rotter! I do not like the man, and I wish my son would have nothing to do with him. Oh, he's a fancier of good horses, and a good enough collector of art. But he's also a collector of women and he uses them shamelessly. He's written a beastly filthy book, filled with all sorts of unmentionable physical practices.

"But for all of that, he's extraordinarily handsome, and being Austrian, he has a romantic, mysterious courtly manner which makes women flock around him like flies drawn to honey. Oh, I just know he's involved in this somewhere."

So saying, the Queen half turned in her chair, averted her face, and touched her handkerchief lightly to her eyes.

"Forgive me, Your Majesty," Holmes asked, "but not having seen your son for three days gave you no cause for concern?"

The Prime Minister, perhaps taking pity on the monarch,

answered for her.

"Mr. Holmes, it is not unusual for Prince Edward to drop out of the public and his family's sight for days at a time. This situation was not, until now, sufficiently different to alarm Her Majesty. Heretofore, at such time as he has become physically and emotionally exhausted, he has returned, full of contrition, brimming over with good intentions to conduct himself more circumspectly in the future. Unfortunately, as soon as he has recovered his health and his spirits, he again goes off on some frolic." Then he added somewhat dryly, "The Prince seems to feel that his sins of omission are of far more importance than his sins of commission."

With the delicacy and tact which characterized my friend when he was dealing with the emotionally distressed seekers of his help, Holmes replied, "I am sure His Grace is well aware of the fact that soon enough there will come a time when his responsibilities toward this land and its people will be such that he can no longer afford his present relatively harmless high-spirited style of living. Our problem here is how to extricate him from his current predicament."

"Thank you, Mr. Holmes, for your diplomatically phrased comment," interjected the Queen, and here we had an indication of the iron resolve lying just beneath the surface of the royal personality, "The heathen already have the bulk of the collection. But we shall never knowingly pay tribute to the Fenians or to anyone else under any threat, under any duress, under any menace, and I am well aware of the consequences of what I am saying."

So am I, Your Majesty, I thought to myself; *so am I.*

"If I may, Your Grace, there are a few conclusions which may legitimately be drawn from this note," said Holmes, and, ticking them off on his fingers, he began.

"First, the document itself is a heavy vellum, a paper which has been manufactured to resemble parchment. It is quite expensive and is, therefore, not typical of what one might expect from an ordinary band of Fenians.

"Second, there are no misspelled words, which in itself may not be unusual, but the style, the choice of words used, the grammatical construction of the individual sentences, all lead one to the conclusion that the author is well educated.

"Third, the writer is a very single-minded, highly disciplined person. This is no hot-headed crusader who seeks redress for all the real or imaginary wrongs perpetrated by the Crown upon its colonies and possessions. No, this man has one cause only - that of Ireland and its independence, and he is perfectly willing to sentence the Prince and Dr. Watson to death if the terms and conditions of this exchange are interfered with.

"Fourth, it was assumed that the first person you would contact regarding this note would be myself, and that I would be summoned to the palace before the day was out. I have no doubt that our arrival here has been observed and already duly reported. It is proper to infer that since Dr. Watson is to be the sole contact, perhaps the writer and his associates have designs upon my physical safety in order to remove me from possible indirect participation. But that's as may be, and I shall have to attend to my own well-being, using whatever means I deem to be appropriate."

"As to that, Mr. Holmes," the Home Secretary interrupted, "we can give you a man from the Yard for protection."

"Thank you, Mr. Secretary," replied my friend, "but we must assume that Watson, and I, particularly, will be diligently watched from the time we leave here until the whole matter is over, and to be spotted with a man from the Yard attending my every activity would surely indicate to the opposition that Scotland Yard is privy to the reason for the shelter afforded by the constable. Sir, I appreciate the offer, but the consequences are more serious than the benefits.

"Fifth, the instructions to prepare the jewels for transport are particularly instructive. Initially, the work is to be completed within a designated time span. I would imagine that the 24-hour limitation begins at the hour of our departure from the palace, because we know that it was anticipated that you would call on me for assistance. But of far greater import is the fact that the money and jewels are to be in 'waterproof, buoyant, shock and salt-resistant containers.' This compels the conclusion of an ocean journey. The specific use of these four conditions strongly suggests the possibility, even probability, that they may be exposed to sea water, possibly by Dr. Watson's jettisoning them at a preselected time and place. Although jewels will not rust, water can be very deleterious to bank notes.

"Sixth, the instructions to Dr. Watson will be by post, as the Fenians would not chance our having 221B Baker Street under surveillance for the apprehension of a messenger.

"Seventh, with reference to the time of delivery and exchange, I believe that making allowances for the vagaries of the postal delivery, it would be five days - or nights probably - from now. How do I arrive at that conclusion? As follows: Today is Monday. The jewels and bank notes are to be ready by tomorrow at this time. We will make an allowance of one day for unforeseen exigencies in packing and for tardiness in post. Therefore, Watson's instructions will arrive by post, possibly tomorrow, but certainly no later than Wednesday. The Fenians will have taken the potential areas of delay into account. So, Watson will have to pick up his cartons, transport them to a railway station, arrange for their shipment under guard as valuable merchandise, under some ruse or another, to some city or village on the coast. There, he must obtain sea transport, and proceed with his cargo in a small boat to some specific location either upon or close to the southern Irish shoreline.

"Eighth, logic compels the conclusion that his destination

cannot be the English coast, because the Royal Navy could seal off the area. His terminus must necessarily be a small inlet on the southeast coast of Ireland where the Navy cannot follow. Once there, Watson either puts his shipment ashore with the use of a dinghy, or he jettisons it over the side upon receipt of some sort of signal. Be assured that the area selected will be quite isolated, and any troop movements, or the presence of any strangers in the area, would be readily apparent to the Fenians.

"And, ninth, the selection of £1 and £5 notes for the currency portion of the ransom, of course, simply is a means of strategy. The use of any larger denominations would be certain to attract attention, and that is to be avoided above all, as far as they are concerned."

My friend paused for a moment, and then added, "Mind you, there may be other equally valid deductions which may be drawn from that letter, but those are the ones that occur to me at the moment."

When he concluded, there was total silence for an appreciable period of time, each of us no doubt mulling over what had been said. For myself, I was never more proud of my association with this remarkable man. To have quickly digested the contents of that message, to have organized his conclusions in such an orderly fashion, and then to have presented them to this small group in such a logical and concise manner was a tribute to the monumental genius of this master of the deductive process. Moments later, my own thoughts were echoed by the Prime Minister.

"Remarkable, Mr. Holmes, absolutely remarkable," he said in tones of near reverence. "But does the message give you any clue as to the present whereabouts of the Prince?"

"Not really, sir," replied my friend. "However, I would adventure a strong suspicion that the Prince has already been spirited away to Ireland. This supposition of mine is not based on anything in the letter, but rather upon the whole bizarre set of circumstances."

This brought a gasp from the Queen. "Those wretched animals! What will they do to him?"

Simultaneously, from the Prime Minister, "How can you say that, Mr. Holmes?"

"I would seriously doubt that the Fenians would have permitted this letter to have been delivered until the Prince was in a place they considered to be safe and secure. After all, they may well have anticipated that Her Majesty would in fact take the precise position she has articulated this afternoon, that under no circumstances would the ransom be paid. In that case they would expect Scotland Yard, the Royal Navy, the Army and the Royal Marines to be thrown into a massive search. There are undoubtedly many, many places they could hide in England, but they are infinitely safer in Ireland.

"We must remember, as has already been noted, that the author of that message has a highly disciplined, even analytical, mind. I have already concluded that Watson is to make his delivery in Ireland, and if we assume that the Fenians really do intend to release the Prince when Watson hands over his waterproof containers, the Prince must be nearby to complete the exchange."

"But, Mr. Holmes," said the Home Secretary, "how do we know they will tender the Prince with one hand, while they receive our ransom with the other, so to speak? Won't they insist on an examination of the shipment to ascertain that we haven't filled those containers with newspapers and cobblestones? Won't the exchange be delayed until they are certain they have the genuine articles?"

"Mr. Secretary," responded Holmes, "I think that is precisely what they will do. And not only that. It is my conclusion that after an examination of the jewels and bank notes has revealed their authenticity, the Prince will remain in captivity for at least another 24 hours to permit those who actually take possession of our half of the quid pro quo to lose themselves in the countryside and to secrete their ill-gotten gains in whatever location shall have been chosen for that purpose. All of which is why I favor the conclusion that Watson will be ordered to either jettison or deliver the packaged booty in the small ocean inlet we spoke of earlier. Again, assuming the Fenians live up to their agreement to release the Prince, I would be of the opinion that he would be put ashore sometime during the early morning hours of the second day after our surrender of the ransom. I fully anticipate that the instructions in the message to be received by Watson will contain some manner of similar language."

And again, a pall of silence fell over the five of us. Probably we were all sifting Holmes' conclusions, trying to find some way around the inescapable. Namely, if the letter was to be literally accepted as an offer of a bona fide exchange of the Prince of Wales for riches worth a King's ransom, and, failing that, the execution of Her Majesty's son, heir to the throne of Great Britain, the Fenians had us in an untenable position. Furthermore, if Holmes was correct in his conclusion that the Prince would remain their prisoner until authenticity had been verified, and secretion in some Irish stronghold had been accomplished, the Crown would have to capitulate.

But we had not reckoned with the lady who occupied the throne, for under her rule, England and the Empire had prospered mightily. I think that at this moment I gained a deep insight into her contribution to our country's preeminence in the world. And, as she spoke, I thought - *this is the stuff of which monarchs are made:*

"Gentlemen, I am truly appreciative of everything which has been said here this afternoon. But let there be no mistake about it - neither the remaining Crown Jewels nor the £500,000 tribute shall be forfeit, even for the life of my son. England has shed blood before, and I have no doubt she shall do so again. But our bloodshed has been for principle and never for personal reasons. And let me assure you that as long as this Queen sits upon the throne of this mighty country, this position is immutable."

In yet another silence which followed, there leaped into my mind four lines from a poem, the name and author of which I have long since forgotten; but no doubt drilled into me by some long-suffering teacher of English literature from my youth:

> "Life is mostly froth and bubble,
> Two things stand like stone;
> Kindness in another' s trouble,
> And courage in your own."

The stillness of the moment was broken by Her Majesty. "Gentlemen, I know you will keep me abreast of any developments as they occur Dr. Watson, Mr. Holmes, I should of course ask you to keep in contact with Mr. Gladstone and Mr. Asquith.

"Now, if you will be so good as to excuse me, I should like to be alone."

With that she rose from her chair, as we did. Our goodbyes were taken and we departed.

In the courtyard before we ascended to our respective carriages, the Prime Minister and the Secretary to theirs, and Holmes and I to ours, we agreed to confer at two o'clock the following afternoon in the Home Secretary's office, selecting the hour as we did for the reason that delivery of the post on Baker Street would occur an hour earlier. Thus it was that my friend and I wended our way to our lodgings in a very thoughtful and somber frame of mind.

Alias Vincent Shannon

Tuesday morning, I was awakened by the sounds of movement in the sitting room, and upon my entry, still in my dressing gown, found Holmes prepared for the street.

"Ah, Watson," he said. "Mrs. Hudson brought some tea, rolls and cereal about twenty minutes ago. I presume you will have to see some of your patients, and there are certain inquiries I should undertake. Let us both make every effort to return by thirty after twelve to meet the post as it arrives." And on that note he departed.

From the window I observed him to stop to have a word with Billy, Mrs. Hudson's page boy, and then he turned in the direction of the City. I made a mental note that he was headed toward Oxford Street, the British Museum, the University of London, and even in the general direction of the Tower itself, although the latter seemed unlikely because of the distance.

After breakfast I completed my ablutions, and set out for my office where I saw and treated several patients. After arranging with Jackson, my neighbor across the hall, to cover my practice for the remainder of the day. I closed my doors about noon and returned to Baker Street. At my request Billy agreed to bring the post immediately upon its arrival. Holmes had preceded me. He was sunk in his chair with his eyes fixed on some point in infinity. I seriously doubt he heard me come in. I picked up the late morning's edition of the TIMES, and thumbed through it idly, looking for any reference to the Fenians, the escaped prisoners from the Tower, the Crown Jewels, or for anything that might be remotely related to the momentous events of the past several days. To my eye, at least, there was nothing we did not already know.

Shortly before the hour of one o'clock, I heard the bounding feet of Billy on the stairs. Seemingly, my friend had instructed his subconscious that this sound, and this sound alone, should intrude upon his trance-like concentration, for with the echoing clatter, Holmes shot upright, saying, "Why, hullo, Watson. That will be Billy with the post, I'll wager."

Opening the door I took from Billy's grasp several items, and turning to Holmes I handed the entire packet to him. Quickly, he rifled through the stack, discarding five or six to the table, and stopping with one letter in his right hand. He was holding an envelope which appeared to be of similar texture to that shown us the preceding day at our audience with the Queen. The printing on its face was to my eye the same bold block style of the message read to us by the Prime Minister.

"Posted at Charing Cross, I see," said Holmes, holding the missive by the margins between the thumb and forefinger of each hand. For a moment we both looked silently at the envelope. Turning to me, he asked, "May I have your permission to open this, Watson?" Upon my nod he held it up to the light, tapped it twice with his left hand, and tore open the margin. Shaking out the contents, and holding the communication so that it was visible to both of us, he read it aloud.

"Dr. Watson -

"Here are your instructions for the delivery of the ransom for your Prince Edward. The boxes, packed as we have previously ordered, are to be shipped as freight, and consigned to Harbourmasters, Ltd. at Pembrey and Burry Port. The cartons are to be marked 'Models' and they may be insured for any sum you shall select, but not to exceed £1000. On Thursday of this week, they shall be placed on the 9:15 morning train from Paddington Station, upon which you shall also travel. You will arrive at Pembrey and Burry Port about four o'clock in the afternoon.

"You shall travel under the name of Vincent Shannon, and you are by occupation an architect and builder of harbours. Upon your arrival at the station, you shall engage a drayman, and you will instruct him to convey you and your cargo to the Rose and Garter, where you shall ask the innkeeper for any messages for Vincent Shannon. You shall be handed further instructions to complete your delivery.

"Remember if any of the security services intervene in any way during this exercise, the Prince and you will be summarily executed.

"IRELAND FOREVER

"The Fenians"

"So, Watson," Holmes said musingly, "for however briefly, you are to become Vincent Shannon It has a certain ironic touch. You, an Englishman to the soles of your boots, are to deliver a priceless treasure belonging to the British Empire to a bunch of Irish hooligans and revolutionaries, and do so under the name of Shannon."

"But, Holmes," I remonstrated, "Her Majesty could not have been more specific. No ransom of any kind is to be paid."

"Quite so, Watson, quite so. And I rather fancy that that good lady has absolutely no intention of changing her mind."

"But, Holmes, what then is to be done?"

"My good friend, the first thing to be done is to take this letter with us to our meeting with the Prime Minister and the Home Secretary. Among the four of us, we should be able to devise an acceptable course of action." Turning away to don his mackintosh and hat, he stopped again with his hand on the door, looked at me, and added, "Our plan may be acceptable to Her Majesty and Her Majesty's government, but greeted less than enthusiastically by His Royal Highness. He may die within the next seventy-two hours but if I were a wagering man, Watson, I'd say the odds are three to two against it."

At our bidding, Billy hailed a hansom cab for us and we left for the office of the Home Secretary.

As we were riding down Bond Street, I was suddenly struck by a remark Holmes had made after we had examined the day's letter from the Fenians.

"I say, Holmes, your comment several minutes ago about the irony of my posing as Vincent Shannon on my trip to the southwest coast is only half of the allegory we have in this case."

My friend turned a quizzical eyebrow in my direction, as he asked, "What do you mean, Watson?"

Knowing that Holmes was truly apolitical, I replied, "The Home Secretary, Herbert Asquith, has one incident in his background that places him in a unique position here. In spite of being elected to the House of Commons from a traditionally Liberal district about the middle of the last decade, he was retained as junior counsel to Charles Stewart Parnell, probably about 1888, in the last of Parnell's trials. It seems that Parnell was brought before a parliamentary commission and accused of condoning political murder. He did spend some time in gaol. Now, here we are - attempting to make an accommodation with the Fenians to free Prince Edward."

"Perhaps history will record the coincidence, Watson. Even the best of men cannot suspend their fate," he replied.

Upon our arrival we found the Prime Minister to be already present. After the briefest of mutual greetings, Holmes delivered both the envelope and letter we had just received to Mr. Gladstone. After both he and Mr. Asquith had studied its contents, the Prime Minister cleared his throat.

"Gentlemen," he said, "Within the last hour I have again conferred with Her Majesty, and again she and I discussed the consequences of our refusal to meet the Fenians' ransom demands. She is just as adamant today, if not more so, than she was yesterday. Our posture must and shall be one of absolute rejection. She has placed the entire matter in the hands of the four of us. We have been given carte blanche to take whatever steps we deem to be appropriate. In short, gentlemen, in whatever action we take, we shall enjoy the total and unstinting support of the Queen. However, when I was ready to bid her farewell, she made one last comment, and insofar as memory avails me, I shall attempt to repeat it to you verbatim.

"'Prime Minister,' she said, 'I want there to be no mistake about this. You may communicate to the Home Secretary and to Mr. Sherlock Holmes and to Dr. John Watson, that if even as much as one single pound, or one solitary additional jewel, is turned over to that band of renegades, I shall have all of you arrested, yourselves imprisoned in the Tower, and tried for the disobedience of a direct order from Victoria Regina. Is that clear, Mr. Prime Minister?' I assured her that it was. And then she added, 'As you are the elected official of the highest station in the Kingdom, Mr. Gladstone, your failure to heed this command from your Queen, or your connivance in evading both its letter and its spirit, would be treason, and upon your conviction for it, I'll have your head.'"

"If any of us entertained any thoughts that the lady on the throne would change her mind, or that we might somehow or other participate in some sort of skullduggery in an oblique evasion of her orders of yesterday," Holmes remarked, "that ends it. Not that I anticipated anything else."

"Thank you, Mr. Holmes," said the Prime Minister. "I was hopeful that someone would see it in the same light as did I. Besides, if I may be forgiven a personal reference, I am rather attached to my head."

In retrospect it is probably to the credit of all of us that no comment was made to Mr. Gladstone's remark.

After a moment I ventured to initiate a dialogue "Sirs, I, too, have a stake in what is being done here and in whatever plan shall evolve from this meeting. Has anyone formulated a program which we should undertake? For myself I am willing to participate in anything upon which the three of you shall agree."

While I had anticipated that some expression would come from the Prime Minister or the Home Secretary at that point, interestingly enough it was Holmes who replied.

"I would like to propose to this conference a course of action which to my mind is the best we can do at this time under the constraints which have been placed upon us. Quite honestly, I did not entertain the thought that Her Majesty would relent on the subject of ransom, and all of my thoughts and energies, since Watson and I learned of Monday's letter to the Queen, have been postulated upon the very attitude she has once more displayed to the Prime Minister.

"The Fenians are expecting Watson and the shipment on

Thursday. If Watson remains in London on Thursday, it will be readily apparent to our opposition that England is prepared to do absolutely nothing, and that we have chosen to reject their demands. On the other hand, if Watson proceeds to Pembrey and Burry Port on Thursday, as directed in today's message, and if we send him with bogus cargo, our deception is quickly going to come to light with rather unpleasant consequences both to the Prince and to Watson. So I propose we undertake our own scheme, which is at least partially within the framework of the Fenian statement, but one which perhaps gives to us more of the initiative than we have at the present."

"By all means, let us hear it, Mr. Holmes. Please proceed."

"At once, Prime Minister. Instead of Thursday, we send Watson to Pembrey and Burry Port tomorrow, Wednesday, by the same 9:15 train We can even send along a man from Scotland Yard to be an unobtrusive observer with instructions to intervene only in an emergency. To implement this project, Prime Minister, I would like to suggest that you use the authority of your office to cause a small four-inch article to appear on the front page of the TIMES beginning with this evening's edition. It would be announced that Dr. John Watson has been appointed by Her Majesty's government to be your personal emissary in a matter of state, which appointment will be of indefinite duration. You are reluctant to disclose the precise duties which will be performed by Dr. Watson, or exactly the nature of its national significance, other than it is of some delicacy involving the Crown. You are confident that you will be able to give a full report on Dr. Watson's contributions to the country within a short period of time. That pursuant to his assignment, Dr. Watson will be traveling to the Swansea area on the morrow. For news purposes, if you are so inclined, you might mention, almost parenthetically, the long association of Dr. Watson with myself. Such an addition would also serve to inform the Fenians that his journey is indeed related to the subject at hand.

"Before his departure Watson should be provided with a letter signed by yourself setting forth the rather unfortunate position taken by Her Majesty, and stating that indeed the government is prepared to consider certain other concessions to meet their grievances in return for the release of the Prince. You might ask them to prepare a reasonable list, one which is capable of fulfillment, and enjoin them to post the same along to Dr. Watson, or to whomever you might so designate.

"Watson shall call upon the innkeeper at the Rose and Garter, advising that worthy gentleman that he is the fictitious Vincent Shannon, asking for any messages for Shannon which he may hold. If the proprietor blusters that Shannon is not expected until the following day, then we may assume that the man at the very least is a Fenian sympathizer, because his reaction will have shown more knowledge than an innocent man would possess. Contrarily, if Watson is handed a letter of instructions without significant comment, the probabilities are strong that he has simply agreed to hold the message for Shannon pending his arrival. In any event Watson will exchange letters with him, Prime Minister, with a courteous request that should the party who delivered the message for Shannon call, would he be good enough to hand him the letter you have written."

"But, Mr. Holmes," inquired the Home Secretary, "suppose the Fenians' instructions for Mr. Shannon, as we call him, have not been delivered to the Rose and Garter by the time Dr. Watson arrives. What then?"

"No, Mr. Secretary," replied Holmes, "that writing is already in the hands of the innkeeper. The Fenians will anticipate that you, acting through Scotland Yard or the local constabulary, will have ordered the proprietor placed under surveillance until Watson's arrival and departure. So I suggest that unfortunate turn of events is not a genuine possibility.

"There is one other thing, however, which must needs be done. As the Prime Minister, my friend is also rather attached to his own neck, and we should additionally make preparations for Dr. Watson's departure from that village immediately. There is no return train from any station beyond Cardiff tomorrow night If the good doctor has to stay over for the next train for London, which does not leave Pembrey and Burry Port until 8:05 in the morning, we may be exposing him to unnecessary risks at the hands of the Fenians.

"I would therefore propose, Mr. Secretary, that you use your good offices with the railroad to the end that an extra train crew accompany the 9:15 tomorrow, and after our Mr. Shannon picks up his instructions, and delivers your letter, Prime Minister, then that extra crew can transport Watson to Cardiff, where he can board the London midnight express. The accessory railroad personnel can then turn the engine and its one coach around and return to Pembrey and Burry Port, from which it returns to London at 8:05. I believe England's transportation system is under the umbrella of your office, Mr. Secretary."

There followed a silence of perhaps five minutes, which was broken only once, and then by Holmes asking the Secretary for permission to smoke. Quite obviously, all of us with the exception of my friend were critically reviewing his plan in our minds. As one might inspect an expensive objet d'art, we turned it this way and that, inspecting every facet for flaws. For himself, Holmes sat there very much at ease with just the barest expression of self-satisfaction upon his lean aesthetic countenance.

Finally, the Prime Minister rose from his chair, and thrusting his hands deeply into his pockets, looked directly at Holmes for the first time - since my friend had finished outlining his rather remarkable program.

"Mr. Holmes," he said, "your proposal does not, of course,

contain anything which insures the recovery of the Prince in the immediate future. But, I cannot think of a better course of action, and I cannot make any suggestions for improvement. I think you are right. The danger to Dr. Watson is diminished, and, as for the Prince, while he is still vulnerable, he is in less jeopardy because of Dr. Watson's one day journey bearing a conciliatory note. Because of the unalterable stand taken by Her Majesty, we can do little more. Home Secretary, what say you?"

"Prime Minister," the secretary replied, "I join in your assessment of the problem. I, too, support Mr. Holmes' strategy. You are correct, sir, railroads do come under 'the umbrella,' as you phrased it, of my office, and I am sure we can arrange the transportation of Dr. Watson, and the Scotland Yard man, to Cardiff immediately upon delivery of our response to the Rose and Garter's innkeeper."

"Thank you, Mr. Secretary. Notice of the fact of the appointment of Dr. John Watson as Minister Extraordinaire can be released to the press in ample time for its inclusion in the evening and subsequent editions. I shall see to it immediately.

"I do strongly feel, however, that we should have the concurrence of one other person before we set this counterplan into motion. Dr. Watson, what do you have to say? Are you willing to undertake this commission for us, recognizing the danger to which you may be subjecting yourself?"

"Mr. Prime Minister," I replied, "my personal safety would seem to be much greater under the Holmes proposition than under the instructions posed by the kidnappers. If I had been willing to undertake to fulfil the Fenian demands, and I was, these are certainly less exacting. You may count on me, sir."

"Then, thank you, gentlemen," said the Prime Minister, "you shall have my letter by messenger by the dinner hour this evening."

Upon that, we departed, each to his own task in what even then I had begun to regard in my mind as "the Holmes counter-thrust."

Dr. Watson's Journey

The following morning found me aboard the 9:15 westbound train from Paddington Station. I shared a compartment with two other gentlemen. One was tall and broad shouldered, with blonde hair, a short mustache, wearing tweeds and carrying a small traveling case. He was trim, athletic-appearing and business-like, and I assigned him the role of my protector from Scotland Yard. Holmes had, of course, cautioned me before leaving Baker Street to take no notice of a possible bodyguard. I do not believe that the man said a dozen words the entire journey. He read a bit, watched the scenery from time to time, and seemed to nap briefly once or twice. His attitude discouraged attention, and since I had fixed on him as my escort, I was happy to oblige.

My other companion was the direct opposite. He was small, wiry and bright as a finch, in spite of wisps of iron grey hair peeping out from under his cap which he wore the entire journey. Bouncing around on his seat, for all the world like a bird in a tree flitting from branch to branch, he nattered on and on about everything in the world.

His principal interest, I soon learned, for there was little way to avoid the man, was unquestionably race horses. His knowledge was encyclopedic; horses in training, horses currently in competition, horses that were comers, horses past their peak, stallions standing at stud, mares ready to foal, the lineage of all of them, where they had run in the past year, their times, what kind of a track it had been and what odds had been paid. Early on, I put him down for a trainer or bookmaker. When I pressed him as to exactly what he did, he would only say, "I have to do with horseflesh, guv'nor," and that was it. He simply would not be more definite.

Still, with all his entertaining ways and his cheerful disposition, there was something about the man that made me uneasy. There was a hint of lilt in his voice that sounded a touch more Irish than English and this from time to time gave me cause for concern. Still, I thought, in a physical encounter of any kind, my money would be on the bulky Yard type beside me and this thought tempered any apprehension that I felt.

After an otherwise uneventful journey, we arrived in Pembrey and Burry Port at ten after four in the afternoon, only minutes late. I engaged a hansom at the station and instructed the driver to take me to the Rose and Garter. I had the cab to myself, having lost track of my traveling companions upon arrival. The ride consumed about twenty minutes, and I alighted before a slightly faded sign which announced to the weary wayfarer that this was indeed my destination. Bidding my cabby to wait, I entered and approached a young maiden seated behind a small counter engaged in what appeared to be the posting of accounts.

"I beg your pardon, my dear, but would you be kind enough to direct me to the innkeeper?" I asked.

She raised her pretty face from her work and replied, "Sir, I am she. May I help you?"

I coughed a few times to cover my embarrassment and surprise, and responded. "Oh, yes, quite, quite. My name, madam, is Shannon. Vincent Shannon. Do you have any messages for me?"

Without blinking an eye, or giving me a second look, she turned to a drawer in a small desk near her right hand, and removed a packet of letters.

"Shannon, is it? I do believe I have something. A gentleman left a writing for you two or three days ago. He said he thought you'd be along to claim it."

She plucked an envelope from the ten or twelve she had in her hand and pushed it across the counter. I saw instantly that the printing on its face was remarkably similar to the two previous Fenian messages I had seen. Inclining my head to the young lady, I asked, "If I may inquire, did the gentleman say he would be returning to collect any reply I might have for him?"

"Oh, no, sir, he just said to give you the letter when you arrived. "She bent her auburn-tressed head over her accounts again. "And, now, if you will excuse me, sir."

Reaching inside my coat pocket, I drew out the message which had been entrusted to me by the Prime Minister, and placing it on the counter, together with a shilling on top of it, I said, "Thank you, mistress. If you should happen to see the gentleman again, would you be good enough to give him this response."

She murmured her agreement without looking up and I turned to leave. It was then I noticed there were four occupants of the lounge through which I had entered. Two middle-aged, weather-beaten chaps were playing chess in the corner, each with a tankard of stout by his hand. A more senior inhabitant was reading a newspaper, and the fourth, a strapping fair-haired youth in his 20's, was seated in a lounging chair by the fireplace, idly watching the girl. No one appeared to take any particular heed of my departure. When I reached the street in front of the inn, my driver and hansom were waiting, although I noted that a second man, probably one of his friends, was seated beside him. As I climbed into the cab, I asked to be taken back to the station.

Upon our arrival I paid off the driver. His companion remained seated beside him, and although mildly curious, I never got a good look at his face. I strode into the station, and located an official in a railway uniform whose badge identified him as the stationmaster. I made inquiry of him.

"I beg your pardon, Stationmaster, but I believe there is a special leaving almost immediately for Cardiff. My name is Watson."

He looked at me with something approaching awe, and replied, "Indeed there is, Your Excellency. It is waiting for you on track 3. If you will come with me, I shall be honored to escort you."

With that he turned, and with me in pursuit, we walked briskly to the rails, crossed a small pedestrian bridge, and there with its boiler roaring, belching steam, was an engine with its tender, one passenger car and a caboose. The stationmaster handed me aboard the front entrance to the coach, stepped back, gave a signal to the engineer and we were off. I leaned back, slightly out of breath. From the time of my arrival at the station to the moment when the train first began to move, not ninety seconds had elapsed. I thought to myself - when the Prime Minister and the Home Secretary personally take a hand, things happen. They happened so rapidly that our speed was probably close to twenty-five miles before I came to the realization that I was the only occupant of the entire car. My God, I really was being treated like a bloody Minister. My own private train, for upwards of ninety minutes to take me, and me alone, from Pembrey and Burry Port to Cardiff. And what would my dear Mother and Father have said to that!!!

Your Excellency, indeed. I was so lost in euphoria that perhaps as much as half an hour passed before I even thought of the missive from the Fenians now safely inhabiting my inside coat pocket. But it was as if I had heard my friend shouting at me, saying, "Watson, I say, Watson: Will you come off your ruddy daydream and open that letter!"

I removed the message from my pocket, and studied its external surface as I had seen Holmes examine its counterpart two days before It was the same high-quality envelope and the same bold printing that had characterized the preceding messages. Upon its being opened, I found the usual distinctive vellum and again the familiar hand. It read as follows:

"Dr. Watson -

"Acting upon the assumption that you and your freight have arrived on Thursday in accord with our previous directions, we want you to have supper before undertaking the next phase of your assignment. We recommend the beef and kidney pie of the Rose and Garter.

"After you have completed your dining, ask your innkeeper to secure a drayman. One can be readily engaged in the village by one of her pages. Upon his arrival, have your cargo loaded, and direct him to take you to the docks. It should be about a ten-minute ride.

"Once there, you will find an old shanty where the fishermen gather before putting to sea for the night. Arrange with any of the captains to take you and your shipment to Bannon Bay, between Wexford and Waterford on the southeast coast of Ireland. Instruct your skipper that, as he proceeds toward Tintern Abbey, he will see a lantern flash three times on the starboard side. He is to put you and your cargo ashore at that point, and put to sea immediately. When our men have taken possession of you and your merchandise, you will be given further instructions.

"You should, incidentally, be able to hire your captain, boat and crew for no more than £20. This is more than any of them earn in a month of fishing. Do not fear for your safety, for they are honest folk, and if you have come unarmed, and without constables or the Royal Navy to frustrate these plans, you will come to no harm.

"IRELAND FOREVER

"The Fenians"

For a time I sat there and pondered the message and its contents. Certainly all three notes had had the same author. They were written on vellum, the style of writing was identical, and in one form or another, each followed the other in sequence and content. Additionally, each was a masterpiece of clarity and brevity, almost a model for a military dispatch from the battleground, which, I suppose, in a way it was.

I was somewhat surprised by its reference to the price I should not have to exceed for my transportation - not to the amount, because Holmes and I had earlier come to the same conclusion, but that it had been mentioned at all.

Its tenor, too, that I would be in no danger if all their prior orders had been complied with, was, I found, somewhat reassuring. The language could be construed as possibly conciliatory. On the other side of it, however, I told myself, if I, John Watson, thought I was going to receive jewels and notes worth millions, I would show a measure of deference myself. I hoped that there was a full measure of that feeling on the part of the Fenians, because the Prince was going to need all of it.

There was one other portion of the letter that addressed itself to me rather suddenly. Other than a very light lunch, eaten on the way down, my stomach now reminded me quite pointedly that it was long past time to be fed. As if in answer to my thoughts, the door to the coach opened, and a small, wiry man with grey hair peeping out from under his cap came down the aisle carrying a sack. I was thunderstruck! This was my compartment companion of the morning, the race track tout, of whom I had had grave suspicions. Had I, after all, fallen into some sort of diabolical Fenian trap!

Seeing my discomfiture, the man smiled, and extending the sack in my direction, said, "Now, Dr. Watson, don't you mind. I'm Inspector Noah from the Yard, and I'll be around until we get back to London. around daybreak in the morning. In the meantime, here are some sandwiches. They may be cold, but right now I'll give you four to one odds that they'll taste pretty good going down."

He refused my offer to share the food, saying that the engineer had stocked up in pretty good style while he and I had been at the Rose and Garter. When I mentioned that I hadn't seen him there at all, he disclosed that he was the cab driver 's companion on our ride back to the station. He then excused himself, declining my invitation to join me in the coach in our journey back to London, saying that ever since his boyhood, he had longed to ride in the cab of a locomotive and he wasn't going to miss his chance tonight.

The rest of the trip to Cardiff was uneventful. We made an easy connection with the London midnight express, and I slept most of the way into Paddington Station, arriving without incident about seven o'clock in the morning.

When I reached 221B Baker Street, I found Holmes

already gone, leaving me a note to meet him at the office of the Home Secretary at ten o'clock. This gave me time for a bite of breakfast, and to perform the obligatory lavatory tasks before leaving for our appointment.

The meeting itself, again with just the four of us, produced little in the way of a plan for action. I suppose that, with the exception of Holmes, the rest of us spent some of our mental energies trying to fathom just how my friend had so completely anticipated the contents of my instructions. Holmes, himself, was unusually silent. He listened to the rest of us quite courteously as we commented and speculated on the whole sequence of events, but his usual incisive manner was lacking. About an hour before noon, we took our leave. Mr. Gladstone promised to call upon the Queen to acquaint her with the latest developments. We were all, including Holmes, pretty much in agreement that there was little we could do until we heard from the Fenians - if we heard from them at all.

As we left Mr. Asquith's office, I noticed that the clouds had begun to gather and the air was noticeably cooler. I turned to my friend.

"Holmes, is there any way I can assist you in this investigation this afternoon? If there is, you may, of course, count on me. But if there is not, I think I should go to my offices. I need to learn of any problems Jackson may have had with my patients, and, perhaps, to treat some of the ill and the lame."

There was a brief pause before my friend replied. "No, Watson, there are several things I need to do before the sun sets. I want to go to the Tower again. I need some time at the University library, and I'm going to have a try at finding 'Sparrow.'"

I remembered the man he called Sparrow. He was an ex-convict who knew most of what was going on in underworld circles in and around the city. Holmes had used him before, and

Sparrow was a nickname Holmes had given him because of my friend's remarkable ability in persuading this worthy to talk about the comings, goings and doings of the criminal element. So, we parted, I to my medical offices, and he to pursue his investigative talents.

The Explosion
in the Fog

That evening, Holmes was singularly uncommunicative, and even though many questions without answers were swirling around in my mind, my friend had withdrawn into himself. This was a sure sign that he was awaiting some portentous event. My attempts to engage him in conversation were met with monosyllabic responses or were ignored completely.

It was a foggy night without, the beginning of one of London's celebrated pea soupers. It was altogether a good evening for being indoors with a lusty blaze crackling in the fireplace. Although the gas lamps in the street had been lit, they were fighting a losing battle against the inhibiting effect of the fog. The cones of illumination they provided ebbed and flowed with the slowly drifting mists. It occurred to me that in the atmosphere of the events of the last few days, this was a night to invite intrigue and danger.

I joined Holmes at the window overlooking Baker Street. After a time I became aware that his attention was fixed upon a dark corner of the alley to our right. Straining my eyes, I concentrated my scrutiny on that area, and finally I was able dimly to perceive the shadow of a small, stocky lad leaning motionless against the corner of the building. The distance, the vaporous clouds and the almost total lack of illumination made impossible any judgment except of the most general kind. For all that I could tell from our point of vantage, this observer was unmoving and apparently was just looking at 221B.

Abruptly, Holmes lit a candle and placed it in the window.

"Why do you want to call a Baker Street irregular this terrible evening?" I exclaimed.

"There is much truth in your statement, Watson, of which you are not fully aware. In the shadows of a heavy and moving fog, creatures of the night dare. As you said, this evening is terrible, and I mean to protect you from the consequences of it."

He went to his desk where he wrote two notes, placed them into envelopes, and sealed them with a drop of wax. As I heard the steps of the irregular upon the stair, I saw that our watcher across the street had not moved. So much for my initial conclusion!

Holmes passed the two writings to the urchin, saying, "Go immediately to my brother, Mycroft Holmes, at the Diogenes Club, and give the first letter to him. Travel swiftly! Then proceed as quickly as you can to Scotland Yard, and give the second note to Inspector Lestrade. Tell both of them that it is an emergency."

Our courier departed, and as Holmes extinguished the window's candle, I took care to note that the comings and goings of our messenger had not caused our shadow to stir from his position of surveillance. A cold breath of apprehension touched the nape of my neck.

Holmes exited to his bedroom for a few moments. When he returned, he was carrying a small traveling suitcase.

"Watson, this is a night of decision for both of us. I must go on an uncertain journey from which I may not return. My life is in danger because of the knowledge I have. I am pitting my intelligence against the most evil genius our country has seen, against whom our past villains are but ghosts. I fear that your life may also be in peril, and if I tell you more, your activity hereafter would demonstrate your cognizance and comprehension as well. Then, you, too, would be prey to this creature from the bowels of hell. Therefore, as I leave you this evening, do not follow. Bolt the door and shutter the windows.

"If I do not return by morning, look for the man that should be there, but never is. He holds the key. Look for him, but do it carefully. Remember, Watson, a midget standing on the shoulders of a giant can see farther than the giant."

He would say no more in spite of my entreaties. Much of what he had spoken appeared to be a riddle, but it was one which I could not decipher.

Even though I could have reached out a hand to touch him, he would have been unaware of my gesture of support. He stood at the window, a motionless, brooding figure, completely with drawn from the world he and I had shared.

Shortly, a four-wheeled hansom cab pulled up to the front door. The large portly driver looked neither to the right, nor to the left, his elbows on his knees, simply holding the reins loosely in his hands.

Without a word or even a glance in my direction, Holmes turned, picked up his small valise and departed. I heard his footsteps descending the stairs. The front door slammed shut as he stepped outside. He crossed to the carriage, opening the door himself. The oafish driver neither descended from his seat, nor, for that matter, turned his head in my friend's direction to acknowledge whatever instructions Holmes had given him. As the door was closed, the horses were flicked with the reins, and the hansom began to roll forward. A feeling of intense sadness and impending doom swept over me.

Out of the corner of my eye, I took notice of a second cab as it pulled away from the curb some distance on my left, seemingly following the Holmes vehicle.

As the coach carrying my friend reached a location opposite the alley where the observer had been secreted, I saw the latter, a diminutive ghost of a figure, dart out into the middle of the street, and throw an object through the back window of the cab.

Immediately, there was a blinding explosion, and the entire rear end of the hansom burst into an enveloping mass of flame. The rear wheels tottered, wobbled and fell off, and the terrified horses broke out of all control. With the back of the wheelless, fiercely blazing cab striking a trail of sparks as it bounced and scraped along the cobblestones, the remains of the hansom were rapidly drawn to my right and out of my line of sight. Outlined for a moment against the glare of the flame, I saw a boy-sized figure running as hard as he could until he reached the corner where he turned to the right and beyond my vision.

And, lastly, before the entire grim, ghastly and mind-numbing spectacle escaped from my field of observation, I discerned the head and shoulders of Inspector Lestrade leaning out of the right window of the following cab. It is a measure of the volume of his voice, and of the wrenching of his spirit, that, as he too disappeared from sight, I heard his anguished entreaty, shouted to the driver.

"Faster! Faster! After that murderer!"

The Inquiry

Before noon the following day, a police officer rang the bell at 221B with a note from a Captain James, asking me to appear at an inquiry into the preceding night's terrors at two o'clock that afternoon. Certainly I had no desire to relive the enormity of that which I had witnessed, and I knew that my deep friendship for my lost companion would make the procedure doubly trying. But, in spite of a virtually sleepless night, if there was anything which I might be able to contribute to the apprehension and punishment of the person or persons who had snuffed out the life of the world's greatest master of scientific deduction, and my friend, I would endure the emotional strain.

So it was then, at the appointed hour, I made my way to Scotland Yard. After a brief wait, the duty constable showed me to a door bearing the legend 'Inquiry Room.' We entered. It contained a table and several straight chairs, and was otherwise unoccupied. My guide bade me be seated, saying that Captain,

James and 'the others' would be along shortly. For a few minutes I stood and looked out the room's only window. Outside, it was a pleasant day. There were throngs of people in the street, and the waters of the Thames River sparkled in the sun. But I fear the beauty of the scene was totally lost upon me. My grief cast everything in shades of somber grey, and I was unable to respond to what otherwise would have been a lively and stimulating picture.

In a matter of minutes, the door opened and four men entered. A short stocky man with mutton chop whiskers and an unruly head of brown hair, about forty years of age, introduced himself as Captain Hugh James, for the moment at least in charge of the investigation. The tall, distinguished, impeccably dressed, aristocratic gentleman was presented as Sir Lewis Norkshire, representing Her Majesty, the Queen. There was Lestrade and the driver of his cab from the night before. To myself, I noted the absence of the bulky arrogant cabman of Holmes' carriage. But, as distressed as I was, I was touched by the realization that Her Majesty had seen fit to send her personal emissary to participate in the investigation. I thought to myself that somewhere Holmes was chuckling quietly and making some manner of sardonic comment, which only he on occasion could make, but that he, too, was secretly pleased.

After the expressions of sympathy had been made, Captain James placed a box upon the table.

"Dr. Watson, our men have searched what we could find of Mr. Holmes ' cab after the fire was extinguished, and we found precious little of his remains. In another container we have some remnants of a burned skeletal structure and bits of charred flesh which we will release to you for burial, inasmuch as we have been unable to locate his brother, Mycroft. Here are a few less grisly items which perhaps you can identify."

With that he opened the first carton and removed three items.

"These," he continued, "were found several feet removed from the burned-out cab. It is our conjecture that they were blown thence by the force of the explosion. Can you assist us? Do any of these appear familiar?"

I had not realized until that moment that perhaps some faint hope had been kept alive within me that my friend had somehow miraculously escaped that holocaust. But there on the desk before me was the indisputable proof that he too had been mortal. I could identify instantly the bowl of one of his favorite pipes, his badly burned deerstalker, and a charred portion of one of his shoes. Turning toward the window to hide my emotion, I made the required identification.

"Dr. Watson," Captain James began, "as painful as it must be to you, we are most grateful that you have come here to assist us in our investigation of last evening's bombing. Would you please describe to us, in as much detail as you can, everything that you observed?"

"I have already related to Inspector Lestrade the events that led up to the death of my dearest and closest friend. But if my recounting of last night's horror will be of assistance to you, sir, in providing a solution to his murder, I shall gladly oblige.

"He departed our flat without comment and without saying farewell. I was standing at the window and observed him to enter the right-hand door of his hansom. As it drew off, proceeding from my left to my right, a second vehicle, which I later learned was occupied by Inspector Lestrade, came from my left to follow the Holmes cab.

"As my friend's carriage reached a point opposite the alley located to the right of 221B, I saw a small shadowy figure dart out from the alley, and throw an object through the back window of the hansom. Instantly, the cab exploded and burned. I caught a glimpse of the bomber as he ran down the street. He turned right at the corner. Lestrade chased after the criminal in pursuit, and he too disappeared around the same corner.

"As soon as I could will myself to move, I rushed out into the street, but at the site of the explosion I could see nothing except the two rear wheels and some piles of debris burning so intensely that one could not approach the flames closely.

"Although in a state of almost total shock, I attempted to apply the methods of my now deceased friend. I immediately began searching for tracks. I found the footprints of the person who I think to have been the bomber, and I followed them around the corner and to an alley where they vanished. I say 'I think to have been the bomber,' because, for a running man, the stride was quite short and more appropriate to a young lad.

"I found the tracks from Lestrade's cab also going around the corner, and at two places the wheels had run over the footprints, obliterating them.

"Of the hansom in which Holmes had departed, there were but two-wheel trails, and two long skids where the chassis of the destroyed cab was being dragged. Naturally, I saw the marks of the hooves of the horses for each of the respective carriages.

"I observed no other footprints in the immediate vicinity of the explosion, and my mind is satisfied that it is not possible that anyone walked away from that destruction. My friend perished and burned in the carriage.

"I rushed down the street in an attempt to follow the tracks of Holmes' hansom. The skid marks turned around two corners and then completely disappeared, vanished into thin air.

"I have nothing else to add. I have given you a full and complete account of what I saw and did last evening just before, and immediately after, Holmes was killed."

The room was silent for several seconds. Someone sighed deeply.

"Unbelievable, utterly unbelievable," murmured Sir Lewis.

"Dr. Watson," said Lestrade, "my story is even more inconceivable than yours. In fact my superiors give no credence to it."

"Lestrade, I must confess that after hearing Dr. Watson, I am less skeptical of your report," Captain James said thoughtfully. "Please repeat your observations one more time so that all of us may hear them."

"Yes, sir. A street urchin brought a message to me at the Yard from Mr. Holmes. The note read 'Secure a hansom and come immediately to Baker Street. My life is in danger. When I depart my lodgings, follow me closely, but at your peril.' It was signed 'Holmes. '

"When Mr. Holmes' cabman pulled away from 221B, I followed about thirty paces behind in one of the Yard's hansoms. The fog was extremely dense, and we could barely see the lights on his carriage.

"Suddenly, just as Dr. Watson described, a small boy burst out of the shadows from an alley or doorway across the street. As he crossed behind Mr. Holmes' departing coach, he tossed an object through the back window into the passenger compartment where Mr. Holmes was riding. There was an explosion, and simultaneously the vehicle burst into a bloody awful flame.

"I leaned out from my cab and yelled for the driver to follow the lad, as he was even then rounding the corner. We began to gain on him, but as we tried to turn the corner, the horses' hooves slipped on the cobblestones because of the dampness of the fog, and we slid into the lamp standard on the far side of the street, and bent the left front wheel.

"I saw the boy dart into a narrow passage about half way down the block. I ran after him. He turned to his left when he reached its end. At that moment I was only about forty feet behind. As soon as I emerged from the alley, I also turned left, and I suddenly saw his feet - now only about thirty feet away - but his feet were about the level of my eyes! I looked upward and, as God is my witness, he was climbing straight up in the air, almost as if he were swimming. I was so confounded that I just stood there as he swam right up out of my sight.

"When he disappeared - just evaporated into thin air - I ran to the spot where I had last seen him, and could find nothing.

"Following the advice Mr. Holmes always gave us, I then searched the street. I saw a single set of footprints which indicated that the boy had been running. These prints ceased at the point where he began to swim upwards into the fog. I could find absolutely nothing else. There is naught else to report."

At the request of Captain James, Lestrade illustrated the arm and leg action of the youth as he 'swam' away into the night, his left arm and foot moving up and down together, and alternating similarly with the right arm and foot.

"Lestrade," I said, "I would think you insane, except that I experienced a like occurrence with the disappearance of Holmes' cab."

"What do you mean by that comment, Doctor?" asked Sir Lewis.

"In the recitation of my observations of last evening which I gave to you earlier, sir, I mentioned that I had followed the skidding marks of the Holmes carriage. These dragging marks suddenly. vanished, as I told you, after the remains of the hansom had turned two corners.

"But thinking back on that particular event now, in the light of Lestrade's testimony here today, there was one curious phenomenon which probably should be mentioned, although I do not know what significance, if any, should be attached to it.

"At the point those skids vanished, a set of dual wheel tracks continued. I assumed earlier that they were from an entirely different carriage, because of the absence of the drag marks of the chassis. However, a third tire track appeared exactly at that spot. It was positioned approximately in the middle of those two presumably front wheel marks.

"As I say, earlier I had dismissed this happening as being unrelated. I certainly have no explanation for it. But in view of the several mysteries presented in this case, this, if it has any relevance at all, may only serve to obscure an already dusky picture."

Book II:
Of
Independent
Inquiry

I Confer with Mycroft Holmes

When the formalities of the Inquiry were finally and blessedly over, I made my way back to Baker Street. In deference to my heavy heart, Mrs. Hudson prepared a light supper and tearfully withdrew. In her own way, our landlady had been as much attached to Holmes as had I.

The evening paper gave a full account of the explosion and death. It reported the facts of the afternoon's Inquiry, quoting Captain James as stating simply that the investigation was continuing. Accompanying the report of the murder was a second article recounting some of the more memorable events in his life. It was an extravagant tribute to my friend's talents and humanity. It listed several of his triumphs which it was my good fortune to have chronicled for the Strand magazine. No mention was made of his antecedents, stating only that he was survived by an older brother, Mycroft Holmes, a resident of London, and a member of the Diogenes Club. The writer was kind enough to mention my long and close association with my late companion.

I let the newspaper slide to the floor, and slowly surveyed the room. Almost every object stirred the chords of memory and set me reminiscing. There was a mounted emerald tie pin, a gift from Queen Victoria, as detailed in The Bruce-Partington Plans. On his desk, and in use as a paperweight, was a horseshoe which some smithy had forged for Silver Blaze. Hanging from the hat rack, just inside the door, was a short walking stick with a weighted head, often called a life preserver, with which Holmes had been threatened in The Beryl Coronet. The gift of the King of Bohemia, a jeweled snuff box, from the story Scandal in Bohemia, involving Irene Adler, the only woman who had ever bested Holmes, was next to his pipe stand, as was the Persian slipper in which he had kept his odoriferous shag. Remembering that it was often my friend's wont to ponder a problem over a few bowls of this foul smelling abomination, I resolved to fill my own pipe, sit quietly in my chair, and go over each fact in the sequence of events leading to my friend's untimely demise. To my surprise I found the Persian slipper to be quite empty, and, I thought, symbolic of the way I viewed my life at that moment. For a time I considered escaping London and the dire drama in which I was an unwilling actor. A great melancholia gripped me, and for several moments all I desired was to attempt to flee the weight of my grief.

But, as I sat there, lighting and relighting my pipe, filled with my own mix, I found my mood gradually shifting from distress to the beginnings of anger, aroused by the brutal and meaningless murder of the finest man I had ever known.

With a conscious effort I began to review each of the bits of evidence of which to date I had knowledge.

First, there was the disappearance of Guri, Ramo Samyi's assistant. Second was the death of Mr. Whitworth, the guard at the Egyptian Hall Theatre. The bombing of White and Wakefield Towers was the third. And, fourth was the bombing death of my friend. An immediate common theme between the latter two was that dynamite, quite a new discovery in explosives, had been the instrumentality used. As it was yet relatively unknown, I began to look favorably upon Lestrade's assessment that the Fenians were the culprits of the destruction at the Tower of London, and quite possibly, I reasoned, in Holmes' death. But what was the connection between the vanished Guri, and the murdered theatre guard, except the theatre itself? Certainly nothing suggested a relationship between those two events, and either dynamite or the Fenians.

It was entirely possible, as it sometimes happened, that Holmes was pursuing two or more independent lines of investigation simultaneously. Life was not quite so ordered and systematic that we could depend upon dealing with only one case at a time. But, if all four of those occurrences were interlocked together, it would take someone with the intellectual powers of a Sherlock Holmes to reason to such a nexus.

It was that thought which handed me a flash of insight. Mycroft Holmes, Sherlock's brother, was in every way his intellectual equal. By Jove, it was indeed a stroke of genius. It occurred to me also that Mycroft might well be in mourning, and perhaps would contemplate leaving the city for a period of time, as indeed had I, feeling that a change in environment and climate would help assuage his loss.

Fearing that he might make his departure without our exchanging our mutual condolences, I immediately arose, retrieved my coat and hat from the rack by the door, and set out for the Diogenes Club.

The Diogenes Club, of which Mycroft Holmes had been a founder, was probably the most unique of all the unique gentlemen' s clubs in London, a city famous for institutions of its kind. The club was established to provide a quiet and comfortable, even luxurious, atmosphere for its members to enjoy solitary pursuits, such as reading and silent meditation.

In the club chambers, speech was prohibited to everyone, including members, under pain of expulsion. Even in the card salon, a ban on conversation was enforced. Only in the billiard and dining rooms was verbal communication permitted. There was provided, however, a visitor's lounge in which a member and his infrequent guest might confer without violating the rules of the house. As my late friend had observed in The Greek Interpreter, the Diogenes Club was created for the convenience of 'the most unsociable and unclubbable men' in London.

Upon my admission into the confines of this remarkable place by the hall porter, I was ushered into the visitor's waiting room. A club steward carried my handwritten message to Mycroft Within a few minutes he joined me.

"Ah, Dr. Watson. I see you have come directly from your lodgings on Baker Street, immediately upon reading this evening's paper. Your presence here is not at all unexpected, sir, and I would suggest that we exchange our knowledge."

Experiencing a strange sensation of Déjà vu, I knew that my decision to seek out Holmes' older brother had been correct.

"How did you know I had just come from Baker Street?"

"There are a few shreds of fresh tobacco of your own mix upon your left sleeve. That tells me that at least a portion of your last pipe was smoked at home while you were seated. Your fingers are slightly smudged with fresh newsprint. I infer that you left your residence almost immediately after finishing your paper. Further, the articles on the TIMES front page would have jogged your memory as to my fraternal relationship, and you would have recalled my small assistances in the past. Your deep friendship with Sherlock would make you want to avenge his death, and I concluded you would seek my counsel."

Giving thanks to the insight which had brought me here, I

proceeded to outline what I knew about my friend's activities.

"Your brother and I were working on four different occurrences. The first was the disappearance of a magician's assistant during the performance of an illusion. While we were examining the theatre the following day, I discovered and displayed to Holmes a rather penetrating list of his interests and disinterests, his strengths and weaknesses. This paper disappeared from under our very noses at about the same time the theatre guard was brutally murdered by a man of prodigious strength. Shortly before this latter incident, Wakefield and White Towers at the Tower of London were bombed. In the aftermath, the Crown Jewels were taken, and several Fenian prisoners escaped. As we know, dynamite was also used to blow up your brother's carriage."

I also related to him the rather bizarre events following Holmes' death, including the disappearance of his coach, and the small statured culprit swimming upward in the air.

Mycroft was silent for several minutes, his steel grey eyes introspectively intent upon the problem.

"Of course, it is elementary to draw a parallel between the use of the dynamite in Sherlock's death and at the Tower. You, yourself, mentioned the vanishing of the conjurer's aide during an illusion. The imagery of the escape of my brother's assassin is also strongly suggestive of a magician's illusion. The strength required to hurl an explosive from the ground through a third story window would be extraordinary, as would the brutal power utilized to rip the throat of the theatre guard from his body. So, what have we? We have dynamite at the Tower and in Sherlock's murder. We have illusions in the disappearance of the girl from the theatre and the boy swimming in air. What is an illusion? It is a deliberately created deceptive appearance designed to invite one to disbelieve one's normal senses.

"Additionally, we have exhibitions of almost inhuman

force in the brutality of the guard's killing and the handling of the dynamite at the Tower. Thus, you have different common denominators running through all four crimes - incredible physical strength at the Tower and the theatre; magic at the theatre and at my brother's homicide, and explosives at Sherlock's death and the Tower again.

"Watson, I assure you, there is something which is common to all four of these occurrences. I am not yet sure what it is, but there are enough common threads to convince me that there is but one answer to all of them.

"Doctor, investigate as would have Sherlock. You must add to all of the foregoing one more fact. The cabinetmaker who built the podium for the Crown Jewels and his daughter have also been found dead with their throats crushed. It is merely another connecting filament in this whole web, in the center of which you shall find the beast responsible for all these malignancies. Return to me here if you have need of further assistance."

My Pursuit Begins

I awoke the following morning resolved to arrange my life in such a fashion that I could devote some time each day to my patients - that was my responsibility as their physician - but determined that the major part of my efforts would be directed to learning the identity of the fiend or fiends who had so ignominiously extinguished the life of my dearest friend. To this end, I decided that my office time henceforth would be in the before-noon hours, and a simple card affixed to the waiting room entry would be sufficient to apprise one and all of that fact. I would leave promptly at twelve o'clock noon, or as soon thereafter as I had completed the examination of my last patient, and after lunch devote the afternoons to pursuing my own investigations. At the moment it did not occur to me that perhaps my services might be utilized by the Fenians or Her Majesty's government from time to time with regard to the possible release of His Lordship, the Prince of Wales.

Thus, for the next several weeks, I found myself almost

totally occupied with these two taxing, but stimulating, pursuits. As I write of my efforts at this point in time, years removed from the actual occurrence of the events themselves, I find myself recalling scenes and vignettes, oftentimes without specific recollection of what had occurred immediately before, and sometimes immediately thereafter. But in order to provide a complete narrative, I have taken the liberty of chronicling some of the various efforts which were undertaken by your scrivener.

The very first afternoon, I called upon Ramo Samyi in his rooms in the Gore Hotel. To the best of my knowledge, there had been nothing new on Guri's disappearance, and now, with Holmes gone, I felt his hopes would have been shattered.

To my surprise he was in fairly good spirits. I learned that Holmes had visited him the day before he had been killed - the day of my train ride to Pembrey and Burry Port. Holmes had had a premonition of impending death, but he had been reassuring to Samyi on the subject of Guri's being found.

"He told me," the fakir continued, "that the investigation was in the best of hands, and would continue regardless of what happened to him.

"So you see, Dr. Watson, in spite of Mr. Holmes being killed, I know the hunt for Guri will go on."

As this was news to me, I inquired, "M. Samyi, did he say who would be in charge of the search?"

"No, Doctor, he did not. He said only that I would be contacted in due course."

"What will you do now? Are you planning to return to your home?"

"Absolutely not," he replied vehemently, "I won't leave London without her. My inner voices tell me she is not dead. She is still alive! I know it inside, and I will wait for her here."

And he struck something of a tragicomic pose, holding his right fist over his heart.

"Very well. To keep you occupied while you are waiting, might it not be a wise thing for you to seek some bookings around the city for some performances?"

"Oh, Dr. Watson, I could not appear without Guri. I may be the one with the knowledge to produce the illusion, but without Guri I am nothing. You see, Doctor, I am 45 years old, she is 22. Her beauty and grace make the magician's simple acts enchanting, and the difficult procedures bewitching. She has a remarkable ability to observe a presentation from the viewpoint of a disinterested and detached professional. She can see things that the most discerning artist would completely overlook. She is much too valuable to me to even consider performing without her."

We talked a while longer before I departed, with mutual promises to exchange information which came into either of our possessions.

My next step was Scotland Yard. Lestrade, and his fellow inspector, Tobias Gregson, whom Holmes had once referred to as being two of the most able detectives on the force, had been assigned the responsibilities of the dual mysteries of the bombing of the Tower of London and the murder of Sherlock Holmes. I spent hours with both of them, singly and together.

I recall conferring with Lestrade on the investigation undertaken by my friend after they abruptly left the Egyptian Hall upon the bombings at the Tower.

"We rode in the Yard's hansom to the exterior entry of Wakefield Tower. Mr. Holmes questioned the Beefeater guards. He was informed that no one had entered or left the Tower since the explosion. In fact, the Tower and the Jewel Room had been closed for the day approximately fifteen minutes before the bomb went off. Thus, the room was empty at the time, although the guards at the entrance were still at their posts.

"Mr. Holmes insisted that all of us remain outside while he conducted his investigation of the Jewel Room. First, before he entered, he stood at the threshold and made a very deliberate visual examination of the room and the destruction inside. Before he entered he made one intriguing remark."

"What was that, Lestrade?"

"He said something about its being anomalous that although the treasures from the display cases in the center of the room had disappeared, all the swords and scepters normally housed in the exhibits in the room's four corners were still present, although lying around on the floor in the debris and rubble. He also commented about the accumulation of glass and dust which had settled all over the fixtures and the floor. He said that from his position in the doorway he could not detect any sign of handprints or footprints. And, as usual, he was right. All the glass in the room had been broken and the dust was everywhere, but one could not discern any disturbances in the coating of the debris to indicate if someone had walked in or out."

"What did he do then?"

"He took his magnifying glass from that velvet case he carried it in, and paying no heed whatsoever to the dirt and rubbish, on his hands and knees, he began inspecting the pedestals and the cabinets. I must say he went over every inch of the floor, and he took his time doing it. You know how he was."

"Yes. Did he say anything?"

"Not until he was done and he came out. He asked the Captain of the guards to safeguard that room night and day, just as though the entire collection was still there, because, he said, 'The remaining objects are worth a Prince's ransom, if not a Queen's.'"

"Did he do or say anything else?"

"Not at Wakefield Tower. He then had me conduct him to White Tower. The explosion there had taken place on the third floor, and we went up to see the destruction. It also was a total shambles. Mr. Holmes showed me the substantial amount of broken glass inside the room under the north window, in contrast to the very small accumulation beneath the south and east windows."

"What did he say about that?"

"Nothing right then. But when we went back down, we walked around the outside of White Tower, and we found a large quantity of glass and debris on the ground on the south and east sides. It was then that Mr. Holmes commented that the evidence showed that a squib or bomb had been thrown from the walk where we were standing, upwards and through the north window on the third floor. He said the distribution of glass shards demonstrated that conclusively, something about explosion and implosion, but I didn't understand that part. As he said, the bomber must have possessed extraordinary strength and accuracy."

"What else happened?"

"Nothing much, really. We talked to the warders and they weren't any help at all. None of them had seen anything suspicious before the explosion. There was one, who looked to me as though he had spent too much time in the alehouses, who claimed he had seen a big, hulking man, running away in the smoke right after the discharge of the bomb. None of our Yard personnel paid much attention to him, because of his condition.

"So, Doctor, you see when we finished and started back to the theatre where we had left you, all I really knew about a very disastrous afternoon was that the major part of the Crown Jewel collection had been stolen, and fifteen Fenian political prisoners had escaped in two almost simultaneous explosions of dynamite bombs at the Tower of London."

There was little else Lestrade could tell me. We reviewed his recital several times, but nothing of significance emerged.

That evening after dinner, I mused upon the almost superhuman demonstrations of physical power which had come to my attention within the last four or five days, and to which I had been a virtual witness.

First, there had been the massive stage door at the Egyptian Hall Theatre - torn from its hinges as though it were paper. Second, I had seen and examined the injuries to the theatre guard - his throat nearly ripped from his body. Third, the bomb at White Tower - the almost unbelievable physical ability and talent required to heave a dynamite bomb from the ground upwards a distance of about thirty feet through a barred window And fourth, the other victims of the criminal the newspapers had dubbed 'the Crusher' - the night watchman at the warehouse, the royal cabinetmaker and his daughter, Beverly Caldwell and Harold Dornn, the two magician's assistants; all of them dead because of a madman whose strength was incomprehensible to the average person. There was no question in my mind we were dealing with an inhuman force which had been loosed upon a public, which yet had not comprehended the enormity of the danger.

But even after making a tentative deduction - that one man was responsible - for all these unspeakable atrocities - was I any further along towards the solution? All I really knew was that my quarry was a man of unbelievable strength. His identity and whereabouts were just as much a mystery as ever. But find him I must. Lives depended upon it.

Information
at the Library

Another incident comes to mind. I remembered that at noon on the last day I had seen my friend alive, he had said that among his afternoon's errands he needed to undertake some research at the university's library. It seemed to me that with any luck I might be able to learn what line of inquiry he had been pursuing. Once there, I found that Miss Sharon Smythe, the assistant head librarian, did indeed have some rather interesting information. She was an absolutely delightful lady of completely indeterminate age, spinsterish, fussy and precise. If one had commissioned an artist to sketch a portrait of a university librarian, he would have drawn Miss Smythe.

She took me into her office, affixed her pince-nez firmly on the bridge of her nose, impaled me on the direct gaze of her cool hazel eyes, and demanded to know who I was, what I wanted to know, and why I wanted to know it. I recall feeling like I was about nine years old and had just been caught in some sort of miscreant behavior. But after I had stammered and stuttered as to my honorable intentions, she thawed and proved to be quite helpful. She had known Holmes fairly well. He had often been a patron, and had frequently asked her to assist him in locating materials. On that afternoon, he had gone through the back issues of most newspapers, and had made a detailed study of the sea and tide charts of St. George's Channel and the Irish Sea. Even more intriguing was the fact that he had asked her to obtain for him whatever she could find on three men, all Irish.

I had felt a slight tightening of the diaphragm. "Can you give me their names, Miss Smythe?"

"Young man," she had responded frostily, "a librarian does not spend more than thirty years in surroundings such as these without an eye for detail and a memory to match. Of course I can give you their names. One was Charles Stewart Parnell, whose name is familiar to every Englishman; the second was the John O'Mahoney family who, I believe, comes from somewhere in the south-central part of Ireland, possibly Cork; and the third was a Professor of History from Trinity College in Dublin. His surname was MacNeill. His given name was one of those Gaelic abominations, which I do not recall at the moment."

It was immediately apparent that Holmes had been occupied with the kidnapping of His Royal Highness. Parnell, of course, was something of an enigma to most Englishmen. He was wellborn and aristocratic. He was a member of Parliament and a powerful exponent of Home Rule for the Irish. He was an Anglo-Irish estate owner with extensive holdings in County Wicklow. He had even spent time in jail for his agitation on behalf of the Irish farmers against their English landlords. The other two names were unknown to me.

Of course, I reported what I had learned from Miss Sharon Smythe to the Home Secretary immediately. He summoned the head of Scotland Yard's Irish Special Branch. The John

O'Mahoney family did indeed come from the Cork area, where they were wealthy landowners. However, the head of the family was one of the founders of the Irish Republican Brotherhood, the predecessor of the Fenians. It was a secret society, whose sole major objective was the overthrow of the English presence by force and violence. His sons were believed to be equally dedicated to that end.

Professor Eoin MacNeill and his son had founded the Gaelic League which was not believed to have its roots in blood and terror. They were watched by the English constabulary, but thus far no reason had arisen to cause their apprehension. For all that the Irish Special Branch knew, the Gaelic League was primarily interested in preserving Gaelic art, music and history, and educating the peasants as to their cultural heritage in these pursuits.

It was thought-provoking to have this background on the three men in whom Holmes had shown extraordinary interest. But what did he have in mind? What insight did this information have for me, or for England, for that matter?

The Fenians Again

About a week after the explosion in Holmes' cab, I received another letter from the Fenians. This one, as did the others, came by the post, but had been posted from Waterloo. The envelope was of the same high vellum quality, and there was no mistaking the block printing of the address. I promptly called upon the Home Secretary, and he and I together went to see the Prime Minister. With remarkably little delay, we were shown into his office. I immediately handed over the message. Mr. Gladstone read it aloud:

"Dr. Watson -

"We received the letter from the Prime Minister which you left with the innkeeper at the Rose and Garter. Its contents required action by our council. We have decided to test the good faith of William Gladstone and his government.

"We shall spare Edward's life for the moment. We will release him if the Parliament votes independence for Ireland, complete freedom from all British interference, and withdrawal of all British constabulary and occupational forces.

"Your deadline is two weeks from the date of this letter. We expect a reply within seventy-two hours advising us if the English cabinet will undertake such a commitment. Your reply is to be delivered to the pubkeeper of the Cock and Bull in Greenwich no later than eight o'clock this Thursday. The message is to be addressed to William Hartley.

"As long, Dr. Watson, as you keep Scotland Yard out of this, you will not be harmed. The Prince's life, however, depends entirely upon what England does.

"IRELAND FOREVER

"The Fenians"

Since it was still rather early in the day, I was asked to excuse myself, to return at five o'clock for tea, while Mr. Gladstone and Mr. Asquith called upon Her Majesty with this latest message. Seeking to put the time to profitable use, I walked to Scotland Yard hoping to see either Lestrade or Gregson. The former was out, but Gregson and I had a nice, but unproductive, chat. The Yard had nothing new on Holmes' murder, the bombing of the Tower, the whereabouts of the Crown Jewels or the escaped prisoners, or the disappearance of the magician's assistant.

I returned at the appointed hour to 10 Downing Street, and was ushered into the Prime Minister's office by his secretary, who poured our tea and withdrew. I was told that Her Majesty viewed the act of giving the Irish their independence in the same light as she did the surrender of the remaining Crown

Jewels and the payment of half a million pounds.

"'The scum,' she said, "the Prime Minister reported, "'whether it be the jewels and notes, or the land, it is still a forfeit; it is still a tribute to the blackest of rascals and heathen. My answer before was an absolute no; my answer today is unchanged.'"

They continued giving me as much of the details of the meeting as they could, and while the position of the Queen was unyielding on the subject of independence, it appeared that she was amenable to making some minor concessions, such as land reform, lower taxes, reduction of troops, and other matters which might somewhat appease the Fenians. However, there was to be no major shift of diplomatic policy.

Our discussions lasted until nearly seven o'clock, at which time the Prime Minister asked that we adjourn to permit him to attend a dinner at the Belgian Embassy. We decided to resume our conference at four the next afternoon. At the invitation of Mr. Asquith, I accompanied him to his residence, where we were joined for dinner by his wife and their eighteen-year-old son.

On my way home afterward in the Secretary's carriage, I found myself reflecting on the unpredictability of life. That I, the son of H. Watson, a poor but respectable teacher, should be meeting on two successive days with the leader of Her Majesty's government, and the number one member of his cabinet, and that I should be having dinner with the latter, was indeed nothing short of unthinkable. If my father, alive, had entered his local pub tonight, to announce, hopefully with a certain pride, that his son had had my experiences of the last few weeks, and was meeting again with the head of state on the morrow, his cronies in the pub would certainly have concluded that he had at least taken leave of his senses and was positively daft.

At four o'clock the following afternoon, I presented myself at the office of the Prime Minister. The discussion quickly resolved itself into a general exploration of alternatives which might be acceptable to the Fenians, and thus to keep open the possibility of a negotiated exchange. Many subjects were broached and examined. In the end we had a consensus that the government's offer would be twofold: First, an act of Parliament which would serve to forgive the Irish tenants their rent arrearages for the last three years; and, second, committing the government to make credit available to the Irish at low interest rates which would enable them to purchase from the English landlords the lands they had been farming.

The letter which I would deliver to the Cock and Bull would also contain a paragraph explaining the Queen's outright intransigence on the subject of Irish independence, but asking the Fenians to accept those proposals as being substantial and representative of a new attitude in Her Majesty's government to give greater heed to 'the entirely legitimate complaints' of the Irish people.

Before we adjourned our meeting, it was decided that one additional bit of the official investigatory process would be added this time. Even though the Cock and Bull was in Greenwich, it was still in London, and we should again enlist the services of the ubiquitous Noah from the Yard. He would arrive at the pub no later than seven o'clock on Thursday, and, hopefully, he might observe who picked up the message which I would leave at 30 after seven. He could be shown a series of sketches and pictures of known Fenians and Irish sympathizers in the London area, and if fortune smiled upon us, an identification might be made.

That was our plan and that is what we did. I delivered the letter as I have outlined above. I later learned that Noah had reported that no one had called for the message when the pub had closed Thursday night. Early Friday evening, at the request of the Home Secretary, I retraced my steps to the Cock and Bull. I was prepared to ask the pubkeeper to permit me to reclaim my letter for a moment or so for the purpose of adding a paragraph, and was advised that it had been claimed earlier that day at the noon closing hour. Alas, the only hopeful note in the matter was that the bartering for the person of His Royal Highness was still in progress. His whereabouts was still shrouded in an enigma as dense as any London fog. We were not to have a reply from the Fenians for nearly ten days.

The Prince's
Theatre Companion

In the meantime, a new line of inquiry suggested itself
to me. The Prince of Wales had been at the Egyptian Hall
Theatre with two other men and with three women. The
only name of those present with him that I was at all familiar
with was that of Godfrey Staunton, the world famous rugby
player. I had never lost interest in the sport, as I had been an
enthusiastic participant as an undergraduate. Each day during
the season, I devoured the pages of the TIMES studying the
reports of the victories and defeats of the various English
teams. A quick perusal of the sports pages informed me that
Staunton's team, the Rovers, was even then in Birmingham
for a series of matches with the aggregations of the Midlands
League. I dashed off a note to Mycroft Holmes telling him
what I was about, and accordingly set out from Paddington
station for that city. Before I left London, I had the foresight to
seek out Albert Bray, an old teammate of mine in the days of
the Blackheath Football Club, and presently the rugby coach

at the university. At my request he had given me a note of introduction to the athlete.

I met the young man outside the player's dressing room after the match with Leeds that evening. His team had won and perhaps that made him easier to approach. In any event, we went to the public rooms of his hotel for a pint. He knew about Holmes' death, and I told him that we had been working on the disappearance of the magician's assistant when the Tower was bombed. With assurances that I was attempting to follow up my friend's investigation, and with a strategic application of stout, he gradually relaxed and became more willing to talk to me. It seemed that it was not really an unusual thing for the Prince and Staunton to spend an evening together. They had met two years or so ago, and he could expect to hear from His Royal Highness whenever his team was in London.

On this particular occasion, he had received an invitation from the Prince a few days before the episode at the Egyptian Hall, the substance of which was that the Prince had a box for the premiere performance of Ramo Samyi. He was to bring a young lady of his choice, and Prince Edward would introduce him to a new acquaintance of his, 'a real stunner.' Present in the Royal Loge had been Baron Adelbert Gruner, who had Lady Patricia Anne on his arm; the Prince and his friend for the evening, Susan Spaulding; and Staunton and his London girl, Carla Diane.

"Was she a real stunner?" I asked.

"Governor, I don't know where the Prince found her, but that Susan was some woman. Yes, she was a stunner - an incredible stunner."

He went on to wax lyrical about Susan Spaulding. According to Staunton, she was a beautiful, tall, statuesque redhead, possessed of a smooth, creamy complexion, with a full ripe figure. In his words, she made all the other ladies in the room appear dowdy.

They had enjoyed a pre-theatre dinner at Claridges, had a rousing good time at the theatre, and they had ended the evening, at least as far as he and Carla Diane had been concerned, at the Criterion. Had they all left together? No, the Baron and Lady Patricia Anne had retired first. Then about thirty minutes before closing time, he and Carla had taken their departure, leaving the Prince and Susan still sipping the grape. Well, yes, as a matter of fact, he did know where I could find this Susan Spaulding. During the course of the evening, when the ladies had excused themselves, the Prince had given him Susan's address with the comment that if he, Staunton, wanted to meet some friends of Susan's, she could take care of him. Yes, he had the address somewhere here in his pouch; here it was.

Before I thanked him and took my leave, I informed him that I was attempting to ascertain any possible connection between the Tower bombing and the disappearance of the magician' s assistant, and to that end I was conferring with as many people as possible who were present at either or both events.

I did not have an opportunity to call upon Miss Spaulding for several days. At that moment I did not see that she could shed any further light upon the problems facing me, and I elected to pursue another avenue of investigation.

A Man Called Sparrow

My friend was going to have a try at finding a man he had named Sparrow on the afternoon of the night of his murder. Obviously, he had in mind some line of inquiry for which he thought Sparrow's unique talents might be helpful.

Over the period of years of my association with Holmes, I had learned that criminal intelligence was often available from informers from the underworld community. From such sources, a person, who had their confidence, as Holmes had, could gather knowledge of the nefarious plans and participations of the public's malfeasors. Many of his successes which have been duly chronicled have made reference to his use of men, such as Sparrow, and indeed of his own involvement, appropriately disguised, in the illegal backwaters of English society.

According to Holmes, Sparrow frequented the areas of the waterfront and the Soho. His real name was Jonny Bird, but Holmes had fastened the sobriquet upon him because of his responsiveness to my friend. To this end, I took it upon myself to try to find him. If, in fact, Holmes had talked that afternoon to this worthy, I might learn what inquiries had been made and what information had been given. My first undertaking, therefore, was to walk the streets and byways of those areas, asking the beat constables if they had any knowledge of the whereabouts of Jonny Bird. Most either knew Jonny personally or by reputation. But, unfortunately, no one had seen him for several days, and none knew where he lived.

After three or four days of nothing but sore feet for my efforts, I decided to make direct reconnaissance of the public houses and clubs which promised the best results for my foray into the underworld. However, before I began, I was struck by the realization that in all probability my presence on the waterfront and in Soho, and my contacts with the police officers, had been noted and passed on, to and through those very persons with whom I was most anxious to make contact. What would Holmes have done?

After pondering this question for an evening, I acted upon my conclusions the following day. I located a secondhand clothing store, and purchased an older style, and in some places threadbare suit, a cap and worn boots. I found a black, false mustache in Holmes' suitcase of disguises, together with some lampblack and spirit gum. From a chemist I bought some cotton to stuff in my cheeks in order to change the shape of my face. It was my plan to camouflage myself and adopt some sort of fringe criminal identity as I searched in person.

To give myself some credibility in the latter area, I called upon Gregson at the Yard. I told him quite candidly what I planned to do. As a good officer should, he did his very best to dissuade me, and became very specific concerning the potential personal dangers attendant to my mission. When his efforts failed, from some locker or other, he produced a cosh and knife for my self-protection. He then did me the biggest favor of all, and, as I write this narrative at this later date I more fully appreciate that all of what he did was in large measure done because of his deep sense of loss and respect for the memory of my friend.

He took me down the hall and into another office. He introduced me to another inspector, Geoffrey Churma, explained what I was up to, and asked Churma to spend an hour or two with me instructing me on the art of buying and selling stolen property. I rather suspect Gregson felt that I was not nimble enough in my manual extremities to be a gambler, stealthy enough to be a burglar, quick enough to be a footpad, dexterous enough for a pickpocket, cunning enough for a smuggler, or sufficiently domineering for a panderer. But, in whatever event, I learned more about being a fence of stolen property in two hours with Churma than I had ever dreamed existed. He taught me what was worth buying and for how much, the language of the street, the art of negotiating prices, and, most importantly, when to walk away from a deal. He also told me that Jonny Bird occasionally acted as a broker in these transactions, and that his specialty was fine crystal, although his primary source of income was cardsharping. In retrospect, I truly believe that the information I obtained from Inspector Churma spared me from serious bodily harm at several junctures, and may even have saved my life. There was more than one time in the days that followed when I felt myself threatened by suspicious members of the underworld fraternity, where the wrong word or gesture, the wrong inquiry or response, or the wrong reaction to a tense situation would certainly have subjected me to a severe beating at the very least.

That evening I made my first venture. I had darkened my hair so that its shade and that of the mustache, which I had affixed with the spirit gum, were virtually indistinguishable. I affected a pair of horn rimmed glasses which I had not worn for years. I experimented with balls of cotton in my cheeks, and I donned the just purchased nondescript clothing. The cotton in my mouth made my voice seem entirely different to me and produced a trace of a lisp about which I was somewhat apprehensive. Suffice it to say that this speech impediment led me to no harm during my search, although I did have to reject a few tentative offers.

Thus prepared, I departed from Baker Street about dusk. I had made the decision to begin my endeavor in the Soho. As Churma had given me a list of the public houses and clubs frequented by men of Sparrow's ilk, I, of course, began with these. My procedure was to order a pint at the bar and carefully nurse it along. Just before I had finished it, I would ask the barkeep if he had seen Jonny Bird lately, or if he knew where I could find him. The answers were usually "No," "Not lately," "Who," or "Don't know him." I did get a few inquiries "who wants to know?" or "Why do you want to see him?" When these latter responses were made, I would reply, "My name's Beddington. I can put him in the way of some real fancy glassware. If you see him or hear from him, tell him I'll be at the Stag's Head at closing for a couple of nights." Then I'd throw a shilling on the bar and depart. In a sense it was exhilarating. On occasion I would be followed outside by a patron, often a trifle unsteady on his feet, who would want to pursue the Jonny Bird subject. From most of the latter I could make no inference if they really knew where Bird was, or whether they were simply trying to interest me, and thus persuade me to buy another pint.

But aside from the increased adrenalin flow, the excitement of the investigation, and dealing with men who one knew operated outside the law, I soon found that there were three major problems which were inherent in my activity. First, what does one do with six or eight pints of beer in a single evening? I solved that one by becoming something of an artist at spilling, and by frequent trips to the water closet. Second, and just as serious, I found the beer absorption rate of cotton to be astounding. Also, beer-logged cotton, taken with the natural effect of alcohol on human speech, made a conversation very difficult at times My solution here, which I put into effect the second night, was to pack a supply of it in my coat, and change the stuffing of my cheeks between each public house at which I stopped. This measure greatly alleviated my problem, at least as to its sponge-like effect. The third proposition was the mornings after. Until the noon hour, I was bumbling around, fuzzy and muddle-headed. There was little I could do about that condition. It seemed to be inevitable in the activity. Indeed, I arranged with Jackson, my medical colleague, to take over my practice for five days.

I will not attempt to list all the places I visited, but there were scores.

But, as always, I would end my evening at the Stag's Head. Early on, I acquainted Roberts, the publican, of my search for Jonny Bird, advising him that I had spread the word around the city that I could be found at closing at his establishment. He was really quite a decent fellow, and I always took care to share a pint with him when I arrived.

Even after five nights of the assault on my constitution and attendant search had ceased, I resolved to continue to stop in at the Stag's Head for a few evenings, reasoning that it might require a few days for the information to filter down - or up - to Jonny Bird.

Sure enough, on the third occasion of my solitary pint with Roberts, a thin, short man, who I judged to be about forty years of age, entered, and after looking around, motioned with his head to Roberts. They retreated to the rear of the room, where they engaged in some rather earnest conversation. I quickly came to the realization that I was the subject of their conference from the frequent glances cast my way by the newcomer. He seemed somewhat agitated and nervous about the whole thing, while my barkeeper comrade was, to outward appearances, the picture of serenity. Finally, the two of them approached the small table where I was seated. The publican dropped into the chair opposite me, while his companion remained standing behind him.

"Mister," said Roberts, "you've been asking around for a certain man for several days. This chap here may be able to help you, but he don't want trouble. I told him I think you're all right. I don't think you're law. But I don't think you're what or who you claim to be. I told him that if he wants to talk to you, I'd stay close by if he needs me."

With that he got up and walked over to the counter where he picked up the leg of a chair from the back-bar which he slapped lightly into the palm of his left hand a few times. All this time, the other man had been standing behind the vacated seat watching. Carefully, I reached into my coat pocket and removed my pipe, tobacco and a five-pound note, all of which I placed on the table in front of me in full view of the man staring down at me. His eyes widened fractionally, and some of the tension seemed to go out of him. I asked Roberts to bring his friend a pint, and when it arrived he slid into the chair across from my own.

"Why do you want to see Jonny Bird, guv'nor?"

"Because I once had a very good friend who told me that if I ever needed certain kinds of information, I should find Mr. Bird and he would help me."

My reluctant partner thought that over for a moment. "This friend of yours; he have a name?" he asked.

I took a deep breath and played my hole card. "Sherlock Holmes," I replied and I pushed the five-pound note toward him.

He gasped audibly. He put his hand on the edge of the table and pushed backwards. But he didn't get up.

"Who are you?" he asked in a hoarse whisper.

"My name is John Watson," I responded. "Hopefully, he may have spoken of me on occasion. I was his companion for many years and am the author of those stories about him in the Strand magazine."

"How do I know you are who you say you are?"

"Do you remember when he was killed?" He nodded. "After lunch that day, he told me he had three things he wanted to do before supper that evening. One was to visit the Tower of London. You will recall it had been bombed several days before. Another was to do some research at the university library, and the third was to find the man he had named Sparrow. It was my idea to try to find Mr. Bird to see if he and Holmes had met. Perhaps with everything else I am learning, it may give me a lead to his murderer."

The man opposite me had locked eyes with mine ever since he had sat down. Now, he remained absolutely motionless for what seemed to be several moments. Suddenly, he exhaled a long sigh, dropped his gaze, slumped back in his chair, and covered the bank note with his hand.

"What do you want to know?" he asked.

"First of all, did Holmes find you that afternoon?" He nodded. "Good. What did you talk about?"

"He wanted to know if I had heard anything about the disappearance of a magician' s assistant several days before. I hadn't. He wanted to know if I had any information on who bombed the Tower. I told him that the street talk was that it was the Fenians. He asked me if I had any names of the Fenians involved. I had heard that there was some English toff who was supposed to be almost a midget, who was supplying their money. I don't have a name to put to him. There's also some talk around that some real big bloke - a giant - acts as the strong man for this midget. I don't have a name for him either.

There hasn't been much word on those two for the last week or so, but a lot of the people I see are asking if they are the ones that did in Mr. Holmes."

I told him I had wondered about that too, since I had seen a small figure, which at the time I had taken to be a boy, throw the bomb into Holmes' hansom the night he died.

Seemingly, other than the rumor about the giant and the small man possibly being responsible for the murder of my friend, Sparrow had nothing to offer on the perpetrators.

"Sparrow, did Holmes ask you anything about the explosions at the Tower of London?" I asked.

"He did," he answered, "and to this day there hasn't been a single word about the Fenians who escaped or whether they are still in the country. I simply can't help you there. Not a bit."

As casually as I could, I put the next question. "Did you and Holmes talk about a kidnapping that had taken place possibly ten days before your meeting, Sparrow?"

"Yes, he asked me if there was anything going around about somebody important being kidnapped and held for ransom. I told him no. But since then, Doctor, I keep hearing talk that the Fenians have somebody well-known - maybe even a nobleman. I don't know who it is, or where he is, but I did hear that whoever it is has been taken to Ireland within the last three or four days."

"I have only one more question for you, sir," I said "Can you suggest anyplace - any club, public house - anywhere that I might go where I might hear some gossip on the Fenians and what they are doing? After all, I spent five days looking for you in places I never thought I would ever visit. Maybe I can push my luck the same way with them, if you could give me a clue on where to start."

Sparrow thought in silence for several minutes. Finally, he

raised his head and said, "I don't know where it is, and I don't know the name of it, but I've been told there is a real nobby place - a kind of club - here in London where a lot of toffs and swells and Whitehall people go. They have rooms and real fine women. You get a lot of spirits and food, and maybe you get to talking. But the people who run it pass along to the Fenians everything they hear."

We talked for another half hour, but he just did not have anything more on this 'club.' We parted with his promise to meet me every Tuesday night thirty minutes before closing there at the Stag's Head, and if he learned anything urgent between our weekly encounters, he would leave word with Billy at 221 Baker Street.

That night before bed, I sat down and with pen in hand scored my information to date.

1. The magician's assistant - a clear miss.

2. The Tower bombing - the involvement of the Fenians was not new, but the implicating presence of a wealthy midget, and his strong man - the giant - was.

3. Holmes' murder - those same two as the possible murderers. It wasn't much, but it was more than I had had.

4. The Crown Jewels - simply dropped out of sight; that Sparrow hadn't mentioned them or that Holmes hadn't inquired about them - might be significant in and of itself.

5. A fancy brothel run by the Fenians - frequented by administrators of the government's policy toward Ireland was indeed of eminent import. The problem, however: Where is it? How is one admitted? Would I have to be introduced; if so, by whom? If I were admitted, what role would I be expected to play?

Before I went to sleep that night, the thought crossed my mind that perhaps there might be an enjoyable segment of this investigation after all.

55 Eaton Terrace

It was while I was taking a few days to recover from the excesses of my hunt for Sparrow, and two or three days after my face-to-face meeting with him at the Stag's Head, that I recalled I had never pursued my investigation with Susan Spaulding. The evening's constant demands in looking for Jonny Bird, together with my playing the bon vivant at the innumerable alehouses and clubs which I had visited, had left me physically drained and an emotional reaction had set in. As a physician, I knew a short period of recuperation was in order. Thus, for a few days I did little more than eat, sleep and visit the Turkish baths. Any other waking time was spent in reviewing in my mind what progress, if any, I had made. It was during one of those introspective sessions that I took pen to paper with an eye to finding new leads to pursue and reexamining old ones. In this manner the Susan Spaulding subject came to mind.

After some little search I found the note with her address which had been given to me at Birmingham by Staunton, the rugger. Immediately I posted a note to her at 55 Eaton Terrace, identifying myself as a confidant of Sherlock Holmes, and as having been in the audience at the Egyptian Hall Theatre the night of the Ramo Samyi performance, which she had also attended in the party of the Prince of Wales. I told her that I was conducting an investigation of my friend's murder independently of the police. I asked if I might call upon her at four o'clock two days hence, to ask her some questions that might assist me in my quest.

On the following morning, the post brought her reply in a handsome parchment appearing envelope. The enclosed note was written in a fine and beautiful hand. Not only did the author accede to my request, I was invited for tea at the appointed hour. The nature of her response and the language used in the message bespoke gentility and refinement to a high degree. I found myself looking forward to our meeting with anticipation.

I was somewhat surprised the following afternoon when my hansom drew up in Chester Row, a court of stables and dwellings. When I asked my driver what Chester Row had to do with Eaton Terrace, he told me that I would find a gate in a brick wall at the back of the mews, and when I had passed through the gate, I would be at 55 Eaton Terrace.

"It's a posh place, gov'nor," he said, shaking his head.

As I paid the fare I thought he looked at me somewhat strangely, but since his remark about my destination being "posh" was equally vague, I put both matters from my mind.

I found the locked door at the end of the mews without difficulty, and, as directed by a small discreet sign set in the wall beside it, rang the bell. A moment later the door was opened by a tall, grey haired gentleman, with an erect bearing, clad in the freshly pressed livery of a courtier of Regency times.

In a voice rich and mellow in the tones of the West

Indies, he asked, "Sir, do I have the pleasure of addressing Dr. Watson?"

After I had responded affirmatively, he bowed slightly and said, "Sir, if you will do me the honor of accompanying me, I shall conduct you to Miss Spaulding. She is expecting you."

He stepped aside, and I entered into the most exquisite Elizabethan knot garden I had ever seen. The air was pungent with the bouquet of what seemed to be thousands of plants and blooming flowers, set and nurtured in exact symmetry. I stopped involuntarily, struck by its breath-taking beauty. My guide paused to give me a moment to savor what my senses of sight and smell were appreciating.

"Almost everyone has the same reaction, Doctor. It really is rather extraordinary, isn't it?" he remarked gently.

At the end of a short path, we ascended three steps to an oaken entry, leading into a fairly large, deep carpeted receiving parlor, where my hat and coat were taken. From there, I was ushered into a lovely sitting room, expensively furnished and richly appointed. There was a grand piano in one corner with a violin lying on a draped crimson velvet scarf. A fireplace spread its warmth and cheer in another corner. Walnut framed oil paintings hung on two of the walls, flanking three quarter length mirrors. An elaborate Waterford crystal chandelier provided the illumination, and a deep gold carpet covered the floor.

But as enchanted as I was by the tasteful and colorful room in which I found myself, it paled when a door directly opposite me opened, and a breath-taking young woman, about twenty-five years of age, entered. It was not so much that she was a statuesque, green-eyed redhead, exquisitely gowned and coiffured, although she was all of that. It was not so much that she had a figure all women dream about, topped with a generous amount of rich creamy bosom above her décolleté gown, although her physical attributes were enough to send any man's senses reeling. Rather, it was that, in addition to all these striking features, she projected a presence of prestige, competence, power, and withal a sensuality that was like a blow to the pit of the stomach. Yet, there was nothing cold about this woman. One sensed a warmth, even passion, in her bearing and personality.

What was the matter with me! I was behaving like a love-struck schoolboy!

Three weeks ago, I had been stricken by the exciting, enigmatic beauty of the lovely Indian girl who had been astride the elephant when Ramo Samyi had ordained its disappearance. I had thought Guri was one of the most captivating women I had ever seen.

But this woman approaching me across this warm and attractive room, with her hand outstretched in welcome, took my breath away. I suspect she was well aware of the fact that I was literally rooted to the floor.

In a rich, lilting contralto voice, she said, "Dr. Watson, I'm Susan Spaulding. Thank you for accepting my invitation to tea. I'm delighted to make your acquaintance. Please accept my heartfelt sympathy for the loss of your very dear friend."

I know I mumbled something in reply, but for the life of me, I have no idea what it was. I was still reacting strongly to this distracting creature standing before me. I do distinctly recall, however, thinking to myself that this was without question the most remarkable woman I had ever seen.

(She told me later that my initial attempts to respond to her greetings were so stumblingly disjointed that she had wondered for a moment if I had a speech impediment.)

She bade me be seated, and stepped to the bell pull in the corner. In a matter of seconds, a maid in a French uniform entered, pushing a wheeled walnut tea cart with an elaborate silver tea service gleaming in the lights of the chandelier. The maid bowed and withdrew, and my hostess, in movements as graceful as though she had trained from infancy for just this occasion, performed the ritual of the English afternoon tea service.

I suddenly realized there was a void in the one-sided conversation she had been carrying on, and I became aware that she was waiting for me to speak.

Taking a firm hold upon my imagination and my emotions, I forced myself into thinking along rational channels.

"Miss Spaulding," I said, "I am very grateful to you for consenting to see me this afternoon, and doubly so because of this opportunity to have tea with you. Your invitation made it clear that you are understanding of my sense of loss, and I am most appreciative of the sympathy that your message conveyed."

She bowed her head slightly toward me and said, "Doctor, what can I do to help you?"

"Miss Spaulding, I'm not at all sure that you can. But since my friend's murder, I've been going back over the ground he traveled the last two or three days of his life in an effort to learn why he was killed and by whom."

I continued on in a somewhat guarded vein. Since the only occasion our paths had crossed had been at the performance of Ramo Samyi, we began by talking about his illusions, and, in particular, the non-appearance of his assistant/wife at the conclusion of his presentation. I told her of the magician calling upon us the following day at 221B Baker Street, and his report that Guri had not been seen since. I related the details of our investigation at the theatre later that afternoon, of the substitution of the folded programme note in the basement of the theatre, and the murder of the guard, Mr. Whitworth.

"Godfrey Staunton told me that after the curtain rang

down, your company - I believe there were six of you - went along to the Criterion for some refreshments and a late supper. This sounds ridiculous, I know, but did any of you have any tangible theories as to how or why Guri disappeared?"

"No, Dr. Watson," she replied. "I remember all of us talking generally of it, of course. Someone suggested a lover's quarrel, and perhaps she simply ran out on him. But, no, nothing other than idle speculation." And with just a trace of a smile, she continued, "I do recall the Prince being somewhat upset at not having the opportunity of meeting her. I think he would have liked to have invited her to join us. He remarked on how beautiful she was."

"Miss Spaulding," I said earnestly, "if the Prince values beauty that highly, I can only say that his inclusion of you as a member of his party demonstrates his impeccable discernment and taste."

There was no simpering or coquettishness in this young lady. With a very slight coloring in her cheeks, green eyes dancing, she replied, "What a delightful thing to say. Thank you, Doctor."

We were silent for a moment or two. As a part of my earlier recounting of our adventures at the Egyptian Hall the following day, I had mentioned to her that Holmes had been called to the Tower of London within a few moments after its bombing.

"I can't help wondering," I said, "whether the theft of the Crown Jewels during the explosion has any connection with Holmes' murder."

"I think most people," she responded, "are pretty well convinced the Fenians bombed the Tower. Do you have any reason to believe they are responsible for the murder of your friend?"

I confessed that I did not have a shred of hard evidence

for my suspicion that Holmes was in fact truly apolitical, but, "Nevertheless, I have this nagging question about it."

Her next comment absolutely brought me up short. For a second, I thought I was hearing the voice of Mycroft Holmes at the Diogenes Club no more than three weeks before. She said, "It is interesting, however, that dynamite was used in both the Tower bombing and the murder of your friend. Perhaps that is the reason for this 'nagging question,' as you call it, that you have in your mind."

But this lovely lady still had one other surprise for me, one other observation that made me aware that my initial impression of her abilities had not been in error. "Even stranger to me, Doctor, is the fact that, as yet, nothing has been raised in the press about the Fenians' demands for the ransom of the Jewels. If I were they, I at least would demand independence for Ireland."

This lady was so close to the actual truth that I deemed it prudent to steer our conversation onto another subject. Thus, after I had remarked that perhaps Fleet Street was not privy to all that was going on between Mr. Gladstone's government and the Fenians, I attempted to be very clever, and I asked her:

"Has the Prince expressed anything to you about Fenian terrorism lately?"

Looking me squarely in the eye, she replied, "I have seen Prince Edward only once since the Tower bombing, and he and I did not discuss the subject of Fenian scaremongering."

Her statement staggered me. She could not have seen the Prince for he had been kidnapped the night before the Tower was bombed. She was either mistaken, or she was simply trying to impress me favorably with her acquaintanceship with a member of the Royal family. In either event I could not press her upon the subject, for to do so would be to reveal his kidnapping, and would, in addition, be most embarrassing to her. My admiration for her which was so high just moments ago, slipped a trifle.

Our conversation turned into generalities, and shortly thereafter, I regretfully took my leave. Except for this last incident, I had been totally smitten by Miss Spaulding, and I regretted that I would never have the opportunity of seeing her again. I was therefore more than a little surprised three days later when the mail delivery contained another envelope in the hand of the earlier invitation. In essence, Miss Spaulding said she had enjoyed immensely our afternoon tea and conversation, and perhaps I would favor her, in confidence, with certain of the other investigatory pursuits which I was undertaking at the present time. She confessed she found the entire subject absorbing. If I happened to be agreeable to sharing my adventures with her, I was invited again to 55 Eaton Terrace the next afternoon.

Promptly at the appointed hour, she received me in the same sitting room, and once more I was enchanted by the beauty and grace with which she performed the tea serving ceremony. After we were completely settled, and without preamble, she took me completely off guard, saying, "I hope you will not think any the less of me for this request, but I would like to make our relationship somewhat less formal. I would like you to call me Susan, and, in turn, I should like to call you John."

Of course, I gladly acceded to her wishes, and soon we were chattering away at each other, as though we had been dear friends for a long time. I told her all I knew about the disappearance of Guri and about the murder of Mr. Whitworth. In my recital I included all the things I had seen my friend do, and say, as a part of his investigation. I recounted my back-tracking upon my friend's trail after his death, of my consequent visit to the university library, my conference with Lestrade on the extent of Holmes' examination of White and Wakefield Towers the afternoon of the bombing, and my search for Jonny Bird, alias the Sparrow.

I did withhold everything about the kidnapping of the Prince of Wales, the ransom note from the Fenians, and my participation in the exchanges of the messages and responses to which I have previously referred. During the hour and a half we spent together, she did me the honor of paying rapt attention, seemingly to my every word. Her questions, interposed as they were from time to time, were pertinent and apposite. She was a superb audience.

On only one matter did she give an appearance that she felt there was more I could tell her. Knitting her forehead in a delightfully distracting manner, she leaned forward slightly, and in a voice that betrayed her uncertainty, said, "But, John, dear, I know you were Mr. Holmes' confidant for years. He must have said something to you about his deductions after he had searched the theatre. He must have commented to you regarding his conclusions after his afternoon at the library, his Tower investigation, and his meeting, if he found him, with this man, Sparrow."

"My dear Susan," I replied, "you did not know my friend. Until his analysis had been proved to his satisfaction, he could be, and was, maddeningly close-mouthed. It was his theory that his discussion of a pending case with me, or with anyone, would only result in distractions to his mental processes, because of the comments I might make or the questions that might be asked. He preferred to keep his own counsel in all matters until his mystery was solved and his hypotheses were firmly established. Indeed, I have often despaired at this habit of his, but in it he was unyielding."

She looked at me searchingly for a moment, and then with a radiant smile, said, "It has been stimulating and exciting to listen to all of these things. I guess I'm just greedy to have you tell me more about this remarkable man, and the adventures which you and he so completely shared."

Then, her smile gone, but still with a twinkle in her eyes, she said with mock severity, "But, John Watson, if I learn that you are withholding something from me, I shall make you pay for it somehow."

"My dear lovely lady," I responded, "I think it would be totally impossible for me to keep anything secret from you."

For the barest fraction of time, I was sorely tempted to tell her of the Prince 's kidnapping, the Fenian notes addressed to me, and my part in the responses which had been prepared by the Prime Minister. But, just in time, I remembered our last tea together when she had told me she had seen Prince Edward at some time or other subsequent to his kidnapping. This I knew to be an impossibility, and so I kept a tight rein on my tongue.

Smoothly and elegantly, she rose from her chair, saying, "My dear John, I am afraid you must excuse me, but I am attending a concert this evening, and I must dress."

I mumbled my apologies for having overstayed my invitation, and kissed the back of her extended hand. As I straightened up, she stepped quite close to me, and to my intense surprise slid her left arm around my waist, and gave me an affectionate squeeze.

I am sure I must have exhibited a state of delighted confusion at this gesture of hers. She laughed quietly, deep in her throat, and said softly, "You dear, dear man. You really are tremendously attractive, and part of your charm is you don't know it. You are a true Victorian."

We had been moving slowly toward the door, walking side by side, with her arm still around me. Just before she extended her hand to open it, she stopped, and standing on tip toe, kissed me lightly upon my cheek.

"John, dear, in the late afternoon Sunday, I am a hostess at a charity function in Knightsbridge. Would you like to come by at thirty after eight that evening and share some wine and a cold supper with me?"

My heart leaped at her invitation. Just moments before I had received a kiss from this exciting woman, and I had thought that in this caress she was saying thank you for an interesting two hours and goodbye. But unless my ears had deceived me, she was bidding my return three days hence for an even more intimate visit. Probably no one has accepted such an invitation with more alacrity, and perhaps that is why she burst into laughter at my enthusiastic affirmative response.

I walked all the way to Baker Street that evening without once thinking about hailing a cab. For the first time since the death of my friend, I was possessed of an emotion other than vengeance. For the remainder of the evening I was unable to entertain any thoughts which were not directly related to my having a late evening with Susan on the coming Sunday.

The Third Demand

The mail the following day brought me back to earth with a rude jolt. It had been sixteen days since we had had any word from the Fenians, and here in my hand was the familiar block-printed envelope. Immediately, I set out for Whitehall and the Home Secretary, and the two of us without delay of any kind called at 10 Downing Street. Within minutes we were ushered into the Prime Minister's office. Mr. Gladstone took the envelope from me.

"Still patronizing the same stationers, and still using the same patently disguised hand," he remarked. With a letter opener from his desk, he opened the message. Adjusting his glasses, he read aloud for the benefit of the Home Secretary and myself.

"Dr. Watson -

"Mr. Gladstone and the English government are temporizing. They have known our terms for Edward's release from the very beginning. Lower taxes, forgiveness of rent arrearages for three years, extension of credit - all these are scraps tossed our way by an arrogant and disdaining monarchy in the hope that we shall be so grateful for these crumbs that we permit England to keep the whole loaf.

"Let there be no misunderstanding or mistake. The price of the life of the Prince is independence for Ireland - nothing more, nothing less.

"This is the last communication you shall receive from us. If Ireland is voted its independence by the Parliament no later than twenty days from today, the Prince will be released unharmed. Failing that, we shall send his head to Queen Victoria. If that is what England wants, his blood shall be upon Her Crown.

"No reply to this message is necessary. We shall know by the appointed hour if England has complied.

"IRELAND FOREVER

"The Fenians"

As the Prime Minister completed his reading of the letter, the silence in the room was so complete, the ticking of the clock in the corner was pronouncedly audible. Mr. Gladstone dropped the document on his desk, and stepped to a window overlooking one of the gardens, his hands clasped behind his back. The Home Secretary moved to the fireplace, and with his hand on the mantel, stared transfixedly into the flames. None of us would look at each other. I think all three men in that room were remembering that doughty lady upon the throne, and I, for one, heard her resolute voice in my head, saying, "whether it be the ransom or the land, it... shall not be forfeit, even for the life of my son..."

The Home Secretary finally broke the silence in the room. "PM, with your permission, since Dr. Watson has been associated with Mr. Sherlock Holmes for many years, I would like to ask him for his impressions of the contents of that letter."

Mr. Gladstone slowly turned from the window, and looked at me, saying, "Yes, I, too, would like to hear from Dr. Watson. Sir, what conclusions do you think Mr. Holmes would have drawn from that message?"

I arose from my chair, crossed the room, and picked up the one page of script. Silently, I perused its contents. Think, man, think, I said to myself. How would Holmes have answered?

"Sirs, I think he would say we are but twenty days from running out of time. The Fenians are not interested in further negotiations or counterproposals. They do not even tell us where to send an acceptance - or any kind of communication - even if we were so inclined. There is absolutely nothing conciliatory in their language.

"The tone of their message suggests to me that the author here is not the same person who wrote the other two notes. Its reference to the Royal family and the government is much more peremptory than that of its predecessors. This is an unemotional, chilling promise - not a threat - of a sentence of death to the Prince if we do not accede. The cold-bloodedness of the language of the penultimate sentence of the third paragraph suggests - and I emphasize suggests - that the balance of power on their council has shifted, and that the more temperate voices, such as they were, have lost control. Other than those observations, I cannot add anything, at least at this time."

"Dr. Watson," said the Prime Minister, and I thought I detected a note of admiration in his voice, "I quite agree with your initial premise - that time is running out. I confess that the rest of your analysis had not yet occurred to me, but your summary was masterful, sir, and I believe it, to be absolutely correct. You have, indeed, learned much from your friend. For just a moment there, I thought we were in fact listening to Mr. Holmes."

"Hear! Hear!" from the Home Secretary.

I flushed with pleasure, partially from their kindness, and partially from a sudden realization that throughout my response, I had repeatedly used the first-person plurals - "we" and "us" - as though I were a part of the decision-making process for the country.

"Dr. Watson, we have a very few days left to us. I should like to propose that we three meet again here on Tuesday next at four o'clock. In the meantime, we individually can cudgel our brains, and next Tuesday we shall see if we have gleaned anything from our efforts."

Upon that note we adjourned for the day.

My Late Supper
with Susan

Committing the happenings of this entire adventure to writing at a later time permits the chronicler a sense of objectivity which might be missing if the events were transcribed contemporaneously with the occurrences. Looking back on the following few days from this vantage point forces me candidly to acknowledge that two matters competed strongly for my attention. First was the dilemma in which the nation found itself because of the kidnapping of the Prince of Wales, in the solution of which I had been asked to participate. The second, of course, was my late supper tête-à-tête with the enchanting Susan on Sunday night.

I tried very hard to concentrate on possible ways out of the plight into which the Fenians had place my country, but my mind kept wandering to my anticipations of being with that exciting woman. I confess that imagination soared to impossible heights of fantasy.

Somehow, and ever so slowly, the time passed, and I was

once again admitted into 55 Eaton Terrace at thirty after eight o'clock, Sunday. It was a lovely evening. The air was almost balmy, and one could see stars over the city. I was shown into the parlor in which she and I twice had shared tea by the French maid, who told me in her charming Parisian accent, "Miss Susan will be with you in a moment."

She was as good as her maid's word. She entered the room looking absolutely ravishing, her eyes sparkling and a welcoming smile on her lips. I felt like a bashful fifteen-year-old schoolboy. She held out both of her hands to me.

"John, my darling John. How good it is to see you. My dear, you look absolutely resplendent tonight," she said in that rich throaty voice of hers.

I found my tongue at last. "It is very nice to be here with you, Susan. I must tell you, however, there is one thing that does give me cause for concern this evening."

"I don't understand, John."

"No female human being, Susan, has any right to be as beautiful as you are tonight."

This exchange set the mood for the remainder of our hours together. She led me into her private suite and proudly showed me the rooms. They were markedly feminine, but there was nothing about them that would make any man ill at ease. Her living room in which we were to eat was comfortably spacious. She had laid out a supper consisting of vichyssoise, cold pheasant, truffles and cheese cake. In a silver bucket, there was a chilled bottle of champagne. We chatted gaily over a variety of subjects while we ate the excellently prepared fare.

It was only after the maid had cleared the food, silver and china to the tiny kitchen that we opened the champagne. At her request I filled two long stemmed crystal glasses.

"We must have a toast, John. You first," she said.

After a few seconds' thought, I raised my glass. "I toast the most captivating person I have ever met. May she always remain as lovely." We each sipped. "And now yours, my dear Susan."

A cloud seemed to pass over her brow, and she, too, was quiet for a moment "John, you know I adore you. But tonight, I would like to toast the health of Prince Edward."

I am sure that my heart must have stuttered.

"What an interesting sentiment, Susan. Have you seen His Royal Highness in the last few days?" I asked as calmly as I could.

"No, John, I have not seen him in nearly a month. I told you about that visit the last time you were here. It's just that I have this feeling that he may be in danger. I have a foreboding of impending disaster hanging over the Royal family."

I was watching her very closely during her response, but there was absolutely nothing in her manner, her speech, or her expression to arouse any suspicion whatsoever.

We sat without speaking for a short time. Then fixing her emerald green eyes earnestly upon mine, she asked quietly, "John, something is troubling you. Is there anything you want to talk to me about?"

I was nonplussed. This beautiful woman, who would have graced the castle of any nobleman in all of Europe, had just offered a toast to the health of a kidnapped Prince, and now was intuitively inviting me to talk out a problem with her.

I sat my champagne glass down and took a turn around the room. I was certain she could be trusted, and I wanted to share this burden with someone. Returning to my seat, I pulled my chair closer to hers and took both her hands in mine.

"Susan," I began, "what I say to you tonight must be kept in the strictest of confidences. You must not repeat it to a soul.

Can you do that?" She nodded without speaking. I took a deep inhalation of air. "The Prince of Wales has been kidnapped."

"I know," she breathed.

In my astonishment, I must have grasped her hands sharply. I saw a slight grimace of pain around her mouth. I relaxed my grip immediately.

"What? Where? How could you possibly know?"

"It matters little," she answered, "but I'll be glad to tell you after you have finished what you have to tell me."

"The Fenians claim they have him," I resumed. "If the English government will grant independence to Ireland within seventeen days from now, he will be released. But, without complete autonomy, they mean to kill him."

And so I told her. I talked steadily for nearly an hour, pausing occasionally to organize my thoughts. For the entire time, her eyes never left my face, and her hands never left my hands, except during the pauses in my recitals which she utilized to replenish our champagne, after which she returned them to mine. She posed pertinent questions on occasion to fill in her understanding of what I was telling her. Otherwise, she sat like a stone, her beautiful face grave and concerned.

(A few days later, I realized I had inadvertently omitted my conversation with Jonny Bird. But, otherwise, I left nothing out.)

When I had finished, she looked at me searchingly for a long minute, and then asked, "What is Mr. Gladstone going to do, John?"

"I do not know, Susan. I am meeting with the Prime Minister and Mr. Asquith the day after tomorrow at four o'clock. Perhaps they will have formulated a plan of some kind by then."

"Darling, will you throw another log on the fire, please? It is becoming a little chilly, and we must talk some more."

I did as she asked, and as I resumed my seat before her, a stab of memory caused me to start.

"I say, when I first said the Prince had been kidnapped, you said you knew. How?"

"There is really not much to tell, John," she replied. "Approximately ten days after the Tower was bombed, a gentleman called upon me in the late afternoon. He gave his name as Fitzsimmons, but I did not otherwise know him. You have met my factotum, Rogers, the West Indian gentleman who answers the gate. He is also my bodyguard, and when Mr. Fitzsimmons called, Rogers stayed close at hand until we were both satisfied that I was in no danger.

"This man presented me with a note written by Prince Edward. He wanted to see me, and he asked me to accompany Fitzsimmons, that I could trust him. I am well acquainted with the Prince's handwriting, and the message was unquestionably genuine. I told Rogers I would be going out for the early evening, and Mr. Fitzsimmons and I departed in his carriage. We were driven to the Greenwich area, and I was admitted to an older home set somewhat back from the road. Mr. Fitzsimmons escorted me into a fairly small and sparsely furnished room which was occupied by two men in masks. I turned around in shock and surprise, but Mr. Fitzsimmons had disappeared. One of the men bade me be seated in the only other chair in the room. They told me they were Fenians, that they had kidnapped Prince Edward and were holding him hostage in one of the upstairs rooms. I would be permitted to see him shortly.

"I was told that initially the price for his ransom had been delivery to the Fenians of the remainder of the Crown Jewel collection and £500,000, but that they were now prepared to accept something else in return for his release. That alternative was independence for Ireland. They - the two men who were talking to me - wanted me to persuade the Prince to write a letter to Queen Victoria, asking Her Grace to suggest to the Prime Minister that the Liberal Party sponsor legislation for that purpose. It was their opinion that if the Queen received such a message from her son, the next in line to the throne, she would do so.

"I saw myself in something of the same position as have you, John. I was an emissary in what I perceived as a vital undertaking, the release of Prince Edward without bloodshed. Thus, I agreed. One of the men accompanied me up the stairs and into a very dingy and bare room. Edward was seated on the floor with his back against the wall. He said he had sent the message to me because he thought he was going to die, and he wanted to see a friend once more. He knew the Fenians would not permit him to have any visitors from his family or from the government. So, he thought of me. I informed him that I was willing to be the courier of a note to his mother in which he could ask her to persuade Mr. Gladstone to propose Irish independence."

"What did the Prince say to that, Susan?" I interrupted.

"He rather shrugged his shoulders and gave me a somewhat sad smile. He said, 'Susan, the old girl has enough on her mind with all the happenings of the last few weeks - the bombing of the Tower, the theft of much of the Crown Jewel collection, the escape of the Fenian prisoners, and my kidnapping. The Royal will is being challenged, and her every instinct is to refuse. I cannot disagree with her. For those reasons I'll not make it any more difficult than it already is, and writing her a letter which begs her to do something contrary to her nature would do just that.'

"And, John, dear, there was nothing I could say to change his mind."

"Like mother, like son," I said softly. "You failed to get his letter, but still they let you go. What happened?"

"He forbade me even to let Her Majesty know he was still alive. Anyhow, I was brought back downstairs, and told that if I contacted Scotland Yard, they would kill Edward and, in any event, they would be out of there within five minutes after I had departed.

"The rest was true. I was brought back here, let out at the mouth of the mews, and the carriage was driven away as though the demons of Hades were after it. I was not able to get a decent look at the driver on the return trip.

"When I told you the first time you were here that I had seen the Prince and that the Fenian movement was discussed, it was the literal truth, John. Prince Edward knew why he was being held, and by whom, but he simply would not discuss it or them. And that is all I can tell you. Now, John, dear, the question simply and solely is: What can be done about it? Or, rather, what can you and I do about it?"

I had listened with single-minded attention to her account of her journey to see His Royal Highness and of her conversation with him.

"There was nothing which would give you any clue of where Prince Edward was to be taken upon your departure?"

"Nothing, John, absolutely nothing! Just that they would be out of there within minutes."

I was convinced that she was telling me the truth. She was as concerned about his safety and whereabouts as any loyal Englishman naturally would be. What should we do now?

"Susan, could you find that house again?" I asked.

"John, I'm not entirely devoid of common sense and a measure of judgment. The very next morning Rogers and I drove out to Greenwich, and we spent the entire day attempting to find it. We must have seen fifteen homes where I could have been. It had been dark as lampblack the night before and the drapes over the windows of the carriage had been drawn. I was fortunate to have been able to have fixed Greenwich as the general location. Now, let me prepare some hot bouillon for us and we can really start to think."

So, for the next three hours or so, Susan and I discussed the ramifications of the latest Fenian letter, the positions of strength and weakness of both the government and the kidnappers vis-a-vis the Prince. We examined the possibilities of innumerable alternate solutions. When we were all talked out, without reaching any answers which we felt had at least a reasonable chance of success, I looked at my watch. It was almost two o'clock in the morning. When I announced my intention of leaving immediately because of the lateness of the hour, I met with resistance.

"John, it is much too late for you to find a public conveyance, and I am not going to disturb Rogers at this hour, to have him take you home in my carriage. We both need rest. I'll get some bedding and you may sleep here on the couch."

I protested in vain, but she would have none of it. She had made up her mind and that was the end of it. I removed certain items of my outer clothing, and pulled an eiderdown comforter over me. In spite of the fact that I could hear the rustling of garments through the open door to her bedroom, probably no more than fifteen feet from where I lay, I fell asleep almost instantly.

It was still dark in the room when something brought me to partial consciousness. Reluctantly, I became aware that someone was gently patting my face, and saying my name over and over again. As I pushed back the curtain of slumber, I realized Susan was kneeling beside the sofa, trying to awaken me. I pushed myself into a semi-upright position, leaning on my elbow.

"John, dear, are you awake enough to understand me?" I nodded dumbly.

"I think I have an answer which just possibly might be acceptable to both sides, and it all may depend on you." Her voice was shaking and she was trembling with excitement.

"For heaven's sake, Susan, what is it?" Her agitation served to push back the barriers of drowsiness.

"You must persuade Mr. Gladstone to propose self-government for the Irish."

"But, my dear Susan, Home Rule has been a subject of debate in Parliament on many occasions. and it has never had a chance." I yawned mightily.

"John, I am talking about something a little different." My head nodded as the desire for sleep kept up its relentless pressure. "Now, hear me out."

I shifted my position on the divan to be less comfortable. "All right. Let's hear it."

"It makes little difference whether one calls it Home Rule or self-government. But this country - this England of ours - has been agreeable to self-government by responsible local administrators for nearly half a century.

"In the late 1840s Lord Elgin was governor general of Canada. He successfully persuaded the Crown that the British government should permit the provinces of Ontario and Quebec to manage their own affairs under one government. Over the years, other British North American territories were merged into the central government, and today we have the Dominion of Canada.

"The same treatment has been accorded to several of our down under colonies. The Australian Colonies Government Act of 1850 enabled, even invited, Tasmania, New South Wales and Victoria to draft their own constitutions, and I believe Queensland and New Zealand have also become self-governing since then.

"So, as you can see, this is not some new innovative concept for Whitehall. Why should not the Irish have the same treatment?"

"But, Susan, are there not vast differences between Australia and Canada on the one hand, and the Irish on the other? Don't these dissimilarities make your idea impractical?" I was still negative.

"I do not understand."

"Well, for one thing, Canada and Australia were colonies of settlement, but they were British colonies. Ireland is not now, and never has been, a colony. For another, Australia is half a world away and Canada nearly so. Ireland is just across St. George's Channel and the Irish Sea."

"Oh, rubbish, John. The colonists who settled Australia and Canada were Englishmen, but they still wanted to establish their own governments, independent of England. And we not only let them do it, we invited and encouraged it. The Irish aren't English. They are Celts, and there's a world of diversity. And as for the distances you speak of, only the English Channel - thirty miles wide - separates us from France and we permit France its own self-government."

"Then, tell me, Susan, please, why is it there has been so much resistance to Home Rule for the Irish?" In spite of myself, I was becoming interested.

"Because the English look at the Irish differently than they do any other English-speaking people. It is an incongruence of attitude Englishmen consider themselves superior to others.

That is why Her Majesty's government could approve the legislation to permit the English colonies to establish their own governments. The Irish are considered to be inferior - shiftless, profligate and of lower intelligence. Superior people must have inferior people upon whom the superiors can work their will, because the inferiors lack the judgment, industry, thrift and intellectual abilities that the English, of course, possess in such abundance. After all, as I said before, the Irish are not English; they are Celts."

Her words echoed the anguished comments of Queen Victoria at Buckingham Palace on the afternoon the first Fenian ransom note had been received. 'Heathen' and 'wretched animals' had been the description then.

"It all sounds very fine, my dear," I said tolerantly, "but are you not asking England to give an entire country away and get nothing in return? Of course, presumably His Royal Highness will be released, but thus far neither Mr. Gladstone nor Mr. Asquith have been disposed to take Parliament into their confidence as to his kidnapping."

"John, now we come to the crux of the proposal. In the middle 1600s Oliver Cromwell became Lord Protector of Britain, which at the time was comprised of three nations, England, Scotland and Ireland. It was a republic and was officially designated a Commonwealth. After he died, we returned to a monarchy, and the use of the title 'Commonwealth' was discarded.

"What you should propose to the Prime Minister and the Home Secretary is the creation of an alliance of countries, all of them self-governing, all of them autonomous. Each would retain certain trade privileges, duty-free exports and imports to and with each other, and other commercial and political prerogatives enjoyed by independent nations. I even have a name for it - the British Commonwealth of Nations, in which England, Australia, Canada, Ireland and other nations may be members. What do you think, John?"

"Hmmm," I said musingly. "It would be a completely new

and daring approach to international relationships. It does seem to be a possible way out of our problems."

"Oh, John, it's the only possibility. It can be advantageous to the Irish and to the English. Ireland gets its beloved Home Rule, and England need not let go of the same commercial advantages she enjoys in her dealings with Canada, Australia and New Zealand."

"My dear," I replied, in my turn caressing her cheek, "you may be the one who has shown us a path to take us out of this dilemma, and, in doing so, save the Prince's life. Of course, the Prime Minister and the government will have to approve, but you may depend on me to utilize all my abilities of advocacy and persuasion."

"There is just one thing, John. When you deal with the Prime Minister and the Home Secretary, this suggestion is your idea and yours alone."

My remonstrations with her upon this point were completely unavailing. I felt she should have the credit for what might prove to be a diplomatic coup.

"No, John, it is important that this proposal be yours. I could not have conceived it, but for our discussions last night. Until now, this whole matter has been one of confidence among what began as the four of you men, and they trust you. Anyhow, what chance do you think this plan would have if they knew it was the brainchild of a woman?"

Her logic was unassailable, and marveling at this beautiful, astute and perspicacious woman, I agreed. In sheer delight, she threw herself into my arms, murmuring, "My darling John, you are irreplaceable. Between us, we could retake America."

I left 55 Eaton Terrace about nine o'clock. It was a bright, sunshiny morning. The birds were singing and London never looked better. For the first time since the death of my friend, I felt glad to be alive. I was more than happy. I was exuberant.

Before I had departed, that incredible redhead of mine had brewed tea for us, and had served some buttered toast and marmalade. Just as I was going out the door, she hugged me once again, and looking into my eyes with mock seriousness, said, "John, my love, when I said last night that you and I together could retake America, I was wrong. What I should have said was 'If you, John, were Mark Anthony, and I were Cleopatra, together we could have conquered the world.'"

I have no recollection of having my feet touch the ground on my way home. I found myself in Oxford Street before I even thought of hailing a hansom. I was in a state of total euphoria, somewhere between the Cloud of the Sublime and the Fog of the Ridiculous.

The Watson Plan

I was still wearing a fatuous smile Tuesday after lunch as I readied myself for my meeting with the Prime Minister and the Home Secretary. At the appointed hour, I called at 10 Downing Street. The sky was overcast and there was a chill in the air. Since I had arrived a few minutes before the Home Secretary, I was shown into the anteroom. It was rather austerely appointed, but comfortable enough, although its furnishings seemed to fit the mood of the weather outside. From a window looking out upon the street, I witnessed Mr. Asquith's arrival. Within minutes the two of us were invited into Mr. Gladstone's chambers. In deference to the threat of rain, a fire was attempting to dispel the gloom of the outside. Once the usual amenities were out of the way, we got down to business.

"Gentlemen, all three of us know why we are here," the Prime Minister said. "Let us begin. I would like to hear first from Dr. Watson and then from the Home Secretary."

"Prime Minister," I responded, "in all deference to you both, I am here by your sufferance only because of my long association with Sherlock Holmes. I am not a member of the government. I do have a suggestion to urge upon you, but because of my status, perhaps you two gentlemen should have the first opportunity to express your respective conclusions."

"Your position is well taken, Doctor. Mr. Asquith, may we hear from you, please?"

"P.M., I really do not have anything that will pull the magical rabbit out of the hat. We have fifteen days remaining. My recommendation is really rather pedestrian. I propose we mobilize Scotland Yard, the local constabularies around the country, the Army, Navy, and the Royal Marines, and launch a massive search for the Prince. Release all details to the newspapers, and through their publishers enlist the aid of the British public. I simply do not know what else we can do, short of giving Ireland away, which Her Majesty will not permit."

Mr. Gladstone nodded his head slowly. "It probably is not surprising, but my thinking has been along generally parallel lines. To your list of agencies, I would add the railway guards and the public hansoms. Post the names, descriptions and likenesses of the major Fenian figures in the postal offices and railway stations. Additionally, the government might establish a reward fund of 100,000 for information leading to the alive recovery of the Prince, said fund to be administered by a three-man commission, whose responsibility would be to evaluate the various data received and allocate the funds to the proper parties. Dr. Watson would be its chairman. I am sure it is all too apparent, Mr. Asquith, that your plan and mine have serious dangers inherent in them, particularly to the person of His Royal Highness. But, seemingly, neither of us has any better, or more viable, alternative."

Turning to me at last, the Prime Minister continued. "All right, Dr. Watson, those are our recommendations. Now let us hear from you.''

"Thank you, sir. Prime Minister, Home Secretary, I have an entirely different sort of proposal to make. Any chance of success it may have would depend solely upon the persuasive powers of you two gentlemen. I do not know if it is a plan my friend Sherlock Holmes would have presented, but, unfortunately, that is something we shall never know."

Then, figuratively putting my tongue in my cheek, I continued. "I can only say that this thought came to me in the middle of the night on Sunday - more accurately, in the very early hours of Monday morning - and unlike most inspirations of the night, I believe this can stand the scrutiny of the light of day."

"Well, Dr. Watson, you certainly have piqued our curiosity," said the Prime Minister. "Let's get on with it."

"Immediately." And I told them in detail - the dual proposal for Home Rule for Ireland, and the establishment of a British Commonwealth of Nations. I used the arguments of history which had been so persuasively pressed upon me at 55 Eaton Terrace, the trade advantages, the duty-free exports and imports, the success of identical policies in Canada and Australia, the political benefits. And I bore down heavily on the far-sighted diplomacy, certainly to be praised by the judgment of history.

"We can withdraw the British troops and the civil service administrators. The Irish can hold their own elections and establish whatever form of self-government they choose, provided they agree to become a member of the Commonwealth. In such fashion, Ireland can have freedom for her people, with no interference from England in the conduct of her internal affairs.

"I also respectfully suggest that such a solution, while perhaps an unpleasant medicinal for Her Majesty, is far more palatable than acquainting each and every inhabitant of this land with the bitter truth that the Prince of Wales was kidnapped six weeks or so ago, and at this time we haven't the foggiest clue as to his whereabouts. If Queen Victoria is reluctant to consent to such a step, then she should be reminded that we have conferred upon New Zealand, Australia and Canada this same self-governing de facto Commonwealth status, to everyone's advantage. So, good sirs, I propose that the cabinet choose the route of Home Rule and Commonwealth."

As before, when the ultimatum had been received from the Fenians, Mr. Gladstone stepped to the window, and Mr. Asquith to the fireplace, and each stood there for several minutes staring at nothing, each engrossed in his own thoughts.

Finally, the Prime Minister turned toward me. "You believe, then, that such action will suffice to cause the release of the Prince?"

"I do not know," I replied. "But I think it has a far greater chance of success than mobilizing the constabulary and the armed forces. Even assuming His Royal Highness is actually physically in England, an assumption which may not be warranted, we would be hunting for a needle in a stack of hay. It would be dependent upon a pure chance encounter, and whatever we may think of the Fenians, we can be sure their conduct will not lend itself to increasing the odds on such an elusive happenstance."

Mr. Gladstone did not respond, but he did return to his chair.

"Home Secretary?"

"Prime Minister," he said, "I really do think it could be pushed through Commons. If the party will support it, then with the votes of the Irish members, you would have your majority. Candidly, what Dr. Watson proposes makes for a better approach to our dilemma than mine. But I would feel a little easier if we had some official authority searching for the Prince. Gentlemen, what would you say to implementing the Watson plan with the Yard's Irish Special Branch?"

"What do you think, Dr. Watson? Do you feel the Secretary's suggestion is compatible with your proposal?" the Prime Minister asked.

"Provided the purpose of the activity of the Irish Special Branch does not become public, I am for it and think it's a good idea," I replied.

"So do I. So do I," said Mr. Gladstone. "The overriding problem is going to be the delivery of the party's vote without an unacceptable number of defections.

He reached into his desk and pulled out two sheets of paper, and as he passed one of the pages to the Home Secretary, I saw it was covered with names.

"Mr. Asquith," he continued, let us each make an independent count of the members we shall probably lose."

For the next ten minutes or so, the only sounds in the room were the ticking of the clock and the scratchings of two pens. The process in which they were engaged was vitally important to the success of 'the Watson plan' - the appellation was flattering - but was a matter totally beyond my ken. Nevertheless, I was well aware of the fact that the result of their enumeration, if seriously unfavorable, might very well scuttle the contribution of my remarkable red-haired young lady of 55 Eaton Terrace. Thinking of her and of our time together less than forty-eight hours ago caused a momentary surge of blood through my veins.

Even as I glanced at the Home Secretary, he looked up from his list. Upon seeing that the Prime Minister had not yet completed his tally, the Secretary turned his eyes to mine. I suppose I might have raised my eyebrows in silent inquiry. Very slowly, he nodded slightly, and raising his left hand, he held his thumb and forefinger about one inch apart.

At that moment, and without taking his eyes from the sheet in front of him, Mr. Gladstone spoke: totals, Home Secretary?"

"By my count, we should carry by twelve votes."

"I make it fifteen," said the P.M. "There are a few names on my list of whom we cannot be absolutely sure, but between the two of us, I feel we can bring them into line."

Turning to me, he added, "Dr. Watson, the Home Secretary and I are agreed that your program can be carried to a successful conclusion. From now on, its accomplishment is in our hands. I would like to say, sir, that Mr. Holmes' suggestion some time ago that you be appointed a Minister Extraordinaire has paid rich dividends indeed. You have been a consistent catalyst in a morass of events, and your counsel has kept all of us on an even keel. Your approach to the entire problem has been statesmanlike. If and when this matter is brought to a satisfactory conclusion, be assured I will acquaint Her Majesty with your not inconsiderable participations.

"Home Secretary, 'the Watson plan' is now our challenge. And, Doctor, you shall be kept informed of any substantive development. We may find that you yet may be of assistance to us, and we shall not hesitate to avail ourselves of your talents and abilities shall that need transpire. Someday a grateful nation may be able properly to recognize your contributions at this hour. Good day, sir."

A Rude Awakening

I returned to Baker Street in a state of exhilaration. On my ride thence, I began mentally composing a message to Susan, detailing my meeting with Mr. Gladstone and Mr. Asquith, recounting their commitment to 'the Watson Plan,' which to my way of thinking should have been named 'the Susan Stratagem.'

Upon my arrival, I found the mail contained an official looking envelope from Inspector Gregson at Scotland Yard. Its contents advised me that the body of Jonny Bird, his neck broken and his throat crushed, had been pulled from the Thames that morning at dawn. Having in mind my inquiries on the street, and in the various public houses and clubs, Gregson voiced a concern that my activities may have had some connection with Bird's demise! He asked to call upon me on the morrow to discuss the entire subject.

I was stunned. If the cause of death had been anything other than that specified by Gregson, I suppose the fact of

Sparrow's killing would not have weighed so heavily upon me. As though I had been poleaxed, some of the various items I had learned began to come together: the murders of the two guards - Smith at the warehouse during the theft of the dynamite and Whitworth at the theatre - both victims had had their throats crushed; the accurate throw of a heavy charge of explosive from the ground upwards through a third story window of Wakefield Tower and the escape of the Fenians; the sightings by the Beefeater guards of a huge man hastening away from the scene in the smoke and mist following the detonation; and, finally, Sparrow's report to me of the street rumors of a giant providing the brawn for a wealthy dwarf, the possible murderer of my friend. Could the news of my contact and conversation with Jonny Bird have been relayed back in some fashion to this monster? Was I responsible for the killing of this rather innocuous, minor underworld figure? My mind was benumbed by the mental associations I was conjuring up for myself.

Moments later, however, I was struck by yet another thought. The picture I had just been sketching was out of focus in at least one respect. If "the crusher" and the midget's giant were one and the same, then Holmes' death was at the hands of a mutant. It was true, dynamite had been used and the explosion had killed him. But the bomber had been small in stature, and there was absolutely no suggestion or evidence that his throat had been crushed or his neck broken. This was contrary to the pattern I had just pieced together. The Royal Cabinetmaker and his daughter, the two guards, the two magicians' assistants, Beverly Caldwell and Harold Dornn - all had had their throats virtually torn from their bodies. Why, then, was Holmes killed by an explosion of dynamite? If the giant had murdered the others at the direction of the midget, why did not the former simply break Holmes' neck and crush his throat? How valid then was my conclusion that these two were responsible for Holmes' homicide? For the first time, I found myself beginning to look elsewhere.

This reasoning - that I had caused Sparrow's death - was so depressing that I could not bring myself to write an account of the day's events to Susan, and I finally went off to bed with my melancholy reflections. Before I finally drifted off into a restless sleep, I attempted to will these passing ideas into sheep jumping over a fence. But, time and again, as soon as I would get the bucolic lambs gamboling in the meadows of my mind, some concept or other would leap into my consciousness, for all the world like a rambunctious ewe or ram, knocking down the palings and scattering slumber to the winds.

The following day, pursuant to his note, Gregson stopped by my Baker Street chambers. I recounted fully my search for Jonny Bird, with the constables on patrol, and my ventures in disguise into the clubs and public houses. I spared no detail of my meeting with Bird at the Stag's Head and of our conversation there.

When I had finished, he asked me some questions which I answered as best I could. He professed to being completely in the dark as to the identity of Sparrow's killer or killers, but he reluctantly agreed that perhaps there was a connective tie between my finding him, our subsequent conversation, and his death.

Finally, just as he was preparing to depart, I thought to ask a question which had been bothering me for over a week.

"Gregson," I said, "Bird mentioned something about an expensive club which caters to the wealthy, which, additionally, is patronized by some of the government officials responsible for making policy on Ireland. What do you know of such an establishment?"

"A little, Doctor, a little," he replied. "It was opened about five years ago. We have some facts and many rumors. Much of it is unsubstantiated. But the stories persist, and most of them have been around long enough that we feel there is probably some substance to them, even though we do not have sufficient evidence to go to a magistrate. What I am telling you is in confidence, but you and Mr. Holmes have occasionally been of some assistance to the Yard. It is probable that Prince Edward and a Baron Gruner, an Austrian, were the organizers, and, at least at first, provided the financial backing. It's for their pleasure and the enjoyment of their friends. We hear that currently it is frequented by some of the peerage and by certain members of Mr. Gladstone's government of sub-cabinet or even cabinet rank. I'm told that the women there are among the most beautiful in all of Europe."

"Have you heard of any connection between this place and the Fenians? What is it called by the way?"

"I heard it once called 'The Hedonics,' but whether that's a name for the place or its members, I have no idea. But, in answer to your first question, there is some suspicion that some of the inhabitants are Irish, and some may be sympathetic to the Fenian cause.

"By the bye, Doctor, in case you were thinking about pursuing another investigation on your own, I'm also informed a person may visit this establishment by written invitation only."

I did my level best to keep Gregson from seeing my confusion. Of course, he had been dead on the mark. I had been most anxious to continue my inquiries by calling at this place for whatever I could find.

"Inspector," I said, "my personal pursuits have not been spectacularly successful thus far, and after what happened to Jonny Bird, I am somewhat reticent to undertake more. Anyhow, what you tell me about invitations would make it rather impossible in any event. For the sake of curiosity, where is this place? It might be entertaining to take a look at it on an afternoon stroll."

"You couldn't see it from the street on a stroll or in a cab," said Gregson. "It is hidden behind a brick wall in a mews in Mayfair. The address is 55 Eaton Terrace."

Gregson made several other comments after that, but I have no idea what they were. There was a roaring in my head that blotted out all thought and sound. I do not know how I was able to stay on my feet. My breathing was constricted and bile rose in my throat. Somehow or other I got through the next few minutes, apparently without Gregson becoming mindful of my plight, because when I finally became aware of my surroundings nearly an hour later, I was seated in my usual chair, and I was alone.

What was I to do? Susan, my titian-haired beauty, that intelligent bundle of sensuous femininity, that alluring, desirable woman with whom I had shared intimacies, was the inhabitant, if not the proprietress of The Hedonics, a daughter of joy in a house of ill-repute! If 55 Eaton Terrace was in truth a nest for the gathering of intelligence for the Fenians, that meant that I had been lured thence for purposes of gleaning from me any scrap of information available which would provide a hint of the plans, specific or contingent, Her Majesty's government had for the locating and rescue of the Prince of Wales. Viewed in this light, it meant that Susan was an agent, and as I could testify from experience, a harshly effective one. I had been completely duped.

But the arachnids which had pulled me into the heart of this web still would not let me go. Perhaps my subconscious had been active just below the surface for days, for I suddenly reached for the two invitations I had received from Susan inviting me to tea in response to my initial inquiry, and asking me again for the same ostensible purpose because she 'wanted to hear more about Holmes and our adventures together.' The envelopes and the letters inside both were of rich heavy vellum which had been woven to resemble parchment. My God! The paper was identical to that which had transmitted the messages from the Fenians, the first to the Queen and the others to me! The ransom notes had come from 55 Eaton Terrace, and I had been too much under Susan's sensuous spell to grasp the connection! No one else had seen the personal invitations. No one else could have seen the nexus. There was no escaping the inexorable fact that I was the only person to have seen both sets of papers.

I was devastated. My mind reeled with the enormity of what I had done - and that which by reason of blindness I had not done. For three days I could function only for the most primitive physical tasks one instinctively undertakes for survival.

The Watson Plan
Accepted

By Saturday morning, however the first signs of returning sanity asserted themselves. I was hungry and I wanted to find out what was happening in the world. I had not read a paper since Wednesday morning before my disastrous meeting with Gregson.

While I was awaiting the hearty fare I had asked Mrs. Hudson to prepare, I removed a three-day accumulation of whiskers and sent Billy out for the daily papers. After fortifying myself with eggs, bangers, biscuits, marmalade and coffee in copious quantities, I lit my pipe and tackled the daily product of the best Fleet Street had to offer. I was searching for news or information regarding the government's activity on 'the Watson plan.' By this time my state of mind had improved to the point that though I still felt like a foolish pawn in a game being played by two crafty opponents, these reflections did not throw me into the deep funk in which I had spent the previous three days.

There was precious little in the print which would have been informative to the average Englishman. There were, however, certain references made here and there to the fact that the Prime Minister and the Home Secretary were holding informal meetings with various members of their party and with some of the Irish members of Commons as well. Any speculation as to the purposes of these conferences was pretty well generalized to 'the Fenian Problem.' Mr. Gladstone had promised a full revelation for the following Monday, when he and his party would propose certain legislation 'which will be of interest to every Englishman.' Such a report would do no more than possibly stir the mild curiosity of the average Londoner, if that. But it told me that Mr. Gladstone's cabinet had determined to pursue the plan for Home Rule and Commonwealth, and that on Monday, the Prime Minister would lay the packet before the House of Commons. It was certain to provoke a stormy debate, one in which the loyalties of the party would be sorely tried. But he and the Home Secretary seemed to feel they had the votes, and the accounts in the press that the legislation was expected on Monday was a good indication that they were still of the same opinion.

In the meantime, what was I to do about 55 Eaton Terrace? About my indiscretions with Susan? For that matter, what was I to do about Susan herself? I really didn't want to see her in gaol, but did not I have a duty as a law-abiding citizen to report what I now knew? Of course I did! But if I went to the Prime Minister - or to Lestrade or Gregson for that matter - and disclosed this knowledge, I would have to confess my improper revelation of state secrets, my scandalous conduct, and my own duplicity. This I could not yet bring myself to do. So, I sought refuge in the time-honored manner of scoundrels everywhere. I temporized. I would reflect upon it further and plan on doing something about it later.

Imagine, then, my utter surprise when later in the day, Billy, our page, knocked on the door, and handed me a letter. The envelope was, of the same heavy vellum texture of the ransom notes. After a moment of shock, I reacted fairly quickly and hailed Billy before he reached the bottom of the stairs.

"Billy, how did this message come into your possession?"

"Sir, a gentleman called to me from a hansom, gave me a shilling, and bade me deliver it to you."

I posed a few more questions, but it was quickly apparent that Billy could be of little help otherwise. He could describe neither the courier nor the cab with any degree of particularity, and, to the best of his recollection, neither had any peculiarly identifying marks.

Closing the door, I tore open the communication with trembling fingers. The message was in the now quite familiar printed block letters.

"Dr. Watson -

"We have learned that you have proposed Home Rule and Commonwealth status for Ireland to William Gladstone for action by the Parliament. This is acceptable to us, provided that all British military and civilian forces are removed from our country within ten days after approval by the House of Commons.

"If these conditions are complied with, Prince Edward will be released on the day following the departure of the last Englishman from the soil of our beloved nation.

"You must communicate this ten day ultimatum to Mr. Gladstone for his inclusion of this condition in the legislation. To that end, we enclose a separate message setting forth this stipulation to spare you possible embarrassment. Being the gentleman you are, we are sure you are anxious to avoid unnecessarily involving others who have served us as well as have you.

"IRELAND FOREVER

The Fenians"

There was in fact a 'separate message' for the Prime Minister, remarkable for its brevity, but devoid of the matters which would have made their recitation trying indeed. It read:

"Dr. Watson -

"You must inform Mr. Gladstone that all Englishmen, military and civilian, are to be removed from Ireland forthwith after the British government grants us Home Rule, but in no event in excess of ten days. This is a condition precedent to the release of the Prince.

"IRELAND FOREVER

"The Fenians"

I read both letters again with mounting joy. The Fenians had given me a means of escape. No abject confessions were required. I could simply take the second note to the Prime Minister, and urge him to include the ten-day demand in his address to Commons, with knowledge that the Fenians were agreeable to Home Rule amid membership in a Commonwealth. They were willing to accept something less than total and absolute autonomy after all! I suddenly felt I was able to discern the fine hand of Susan Spaulding in the entire process. After intensely studying the entire matter for nearly an hour, I came to what I believed to be the most acceptable conclusion: Susan was in fact a double agent. She had generated the concept of Home Rule, and knew that because of her connection with the Fenian movement that she could win their acceptance; that she likewise was aware that I had access to the ear of the Prime Minister, and that the government and Crown would find it easier to accept the ultimate compromise of Commonwealth rather than plenary independence. At that point it became simply a matter of communicating her rationale to both protagonists and convincing each of its merits. Neither had surrendered much of substance and each stood to gain substantially.

With this conclusion reached, my conscience was much assuaged. I began tentatively to justify her conduct on the ground that, indeed, Susan deserved some recognition for her very major part in bringing about a detente between two irreconcilable parties. With a wry mile I observed to myself that I was succeeding in proficiently rationalizing away what just moments ago I had considered conduct of the most perfidious nature.

My burden of right and wrong being sufficiently eased, I called immediately at 10 Downing Street with the second, and shorter, Fenian letter. Upon its being read by the Prime Minister, he raised an eyebrow expressively and observed:

"You know, Doctor, it will not make one tittle of difference to Commons whether the evacuation time is ten hours; ten days, or ten weeks. They will either vote approval or they will not."

And that, as it turned out, was the last time I ever saw William Gladstone.

An Exchange of Letters

I returned to Baker Street, and after several hours of trial and error, starts and stops, drafts and redrafts, I finished and posted a note to Susan. For the sake of a complete record of these unusual events in their entire sequence, I include it here.

"My dear Susan,

"On the chance that you may be wondering just what happened to me after our Sunday night encounter, let me recount the following:

"On Tuesday, I presented as 'the Watson plan,' your proposal for Home Rule and Commonwealth to Mr. Gladstone and Mr. Asquith. As you may have surmised from certain comments in the press, the legislation will be presented to Parliament on Monday next. They believe they have the votes for passage.

"Yesterday the Fenians advised me by messenger that

this proposal is acceptable to them, provided all the English administrators and security forces leave Ireland within ten days after passage of the Home Rule Act. I expect you know about this. Of course, this condition has been communicated to the PM for inclusion in his message to Commons.

"And, now to other matters. On Wednesday of this week, I was called upon by Inspector Gregson from Scotland Yard. In the course of our conversation he told me about 55 Eaton Terrace - what it is, the possible connection of the Prince of Wales, the Fenian involvement, and the collection of information for them. He also gave me the news that a minor cardsharp and small time fence had been murdered, apparently by the same man whose thrown bomb freed the Fenian prisoners from the Tower. The dead man's name was Jonny Bird, and it was he who first told me about your coterie, although he did not know who resided there, or where it was. I am reasonably certain he was killed, because he had talked to me.

"I was shocked beyond description by all this information. I felt I had betrayed Bird, and I felt used by the Fenians and by you - so much so that I could not bring myself to write this letter until now.

"Obviously, our relationship, as pleasurable as it was for me, must be at an end. I am of no further use to the Fenians. But I want you to know that I bear you no ill will. I have not advised anyone of our visits, or of your participation in any of the foregoing events. My conclusion is that you intended, and actually did, provide a service in proposing a compromise, which I firmly believe was your own original concept. It has proved to be acceptable to the Irish and to the Crown. Pray God that Parliament will vote its approval.

"As Pope's Eliosa said to Abelard:
'Of all affliction taught a lover yet,
'Tis sure the hardest science to forget.'

"Farewell, my lovely Susan.
"Your obedient servant,
"John Watson"

True to his word, William Gladstone under the aegis of the Liberal Party, on the following Monday proposed that the Irish be given Home Rule and that the British Commonwealth of Nations be created. There were, in addition to the Liberals, some eighty-five seats from Ireland, who called themselves the Home Rulers. Mathematically, the Liberals and the Home Rulers were more than enough to carry the balance of power at Westminster. The debate was furious. The front pages of the press contained little else. The subject was on the lips of every Englishman, and it was probably responsible for more fisticuffs in the public houses than any other event in the English chronicles. It is a matter of history that when the vote was finally taken, the Liberal Party split badly, and the measure lost by a substantial margin. The following day, upon a vote of confidence, William Gladstone was voted out of office, never again to return. This was the epitaph of 'the Watson plan,' and of the extraordinary ministry I had briefly enjoyed because of the suggestion made many weeks ago by Sherlock Holmes. I was never to receive the formal recognition from a 'grateful monarch,' which previously had been mentioned by one of our country's greatest Prime Ministers.

One last memoir must be added to this narrative to complete this segment of those weeks which followed the murder of my friend.

About seven days after I had mailed my last letter to Susan,

I in turn received a communication from her. It had been posted in Galway, and it read:

"My dearest John:

"I received your note of Saturday last just a matter of minutes before I left for Galway on vacation, and this is the reason for my tardiness in reply. I thank you for your thoughts, as I feel that I, particularly, have an understanding of what the hours preceding your writing must have cost you emotionally.

"I am grateful that you bear me no ill will. Certainly, I meant none toward you. Your assessment of the entire matter has been completely correct. What you have not known is that my Mother was an Irish country girl, and my Father an English nobleman who held estates in Ireland. His name does not matter. It is enough to say that I have roots in both countries which I have endeavored to nourish for many years, and my dear John, you have been a powerful nutrient. I owe no apology to the Fenians for what I may have done for England, and I have no regrets for my ventures on behalf of the Irish. I do ask your forgiveness for any feelings you may have that you have been used. If you were, it was in a good cause, and every minute was a delight. We almost brought it off, you and I; we almost wrote history.

"Regretfully, I must agree with you. Our relationship is at an end - not because either of us truly wants it that way, but because you, a true Victorian as I once called you, could never be completely trusting of me again. Always in the back of your mind, there would be that spectre of suspicion which is fatal to the best of human alliances.

"In future years, when you think of me, and you will, please be gentle, and know that I too will be remembering you with a bittersweet love and esteem. Farewell, my acushla.

> "Affectionately always,
> "Susan"

Sherlock Holmes had had his Irene Adler, the lady he always referred to as "the woman." Now I had mine.

Book III:
Of Truth
and
Vindication

M. Host el Kebar

On the Sunday following the collapse of William Gladstone's government, I rose a little later than usual. My futile investigation into the death of my friend and colleague, and my unavailing efforts on behalf of the Prince of Wales, had drained me emotionally. Too, the failure of the House of Commons to approve Home Rule and Commonwealth status for Ireland had forced me to accept the fact that our endeavors had been in vain, and our hopes for the rescue of Prince Edward had been dashed.

Over a pipe and a cup of steaming hot tea, I opened the morning edition of the TIMES. In idly perusing its pages, I found an announcement that Robert-Houdin's son, Emile Houdin, was to give a performance the following Wednesday evening at the Egyptian Hall Theatre. Recalling my friend's acute interest in all feats of magic and illusion, I read the account with more than a little interest. Robert-Houdin had been dead for years, but he and Holmes had been close friends.

Thus, I resolved to attend, and to pay my respects to the son of this master wizard. The article additionally noted that a new fakir from the Middle East would be introduced to the London audience as a part of the same program, promising illusions never before seen on the stages of Europe.

One can imagine my surprise later in the day when a messenger called at 221B with an envelope containing a ticket to Wednesday evening's presentation. Wrapped around the admission was a note from Emile Houdin himself, which read:

"My dear Dr. Watson:

> "Please accept the enclosed ticket with my compliments. I am most anxious that you should also enjoy the remarkable abilities of my new protégé, M. Host el Kebar, who, I promise, will amaze you in ways I cannot describe. I shall look forward to making the acquaintance of the colleague of the late Sherlock Holmes, the dear friend of my father. Until then, I remain.

> > "Your obedient servant,
> > "Emile Houdin"

On Wednesday evening I dined early and set out for the Egyptian Hall, arriving about twenty minutes before curtain time. A page conducted me to my loge, and, as I seated myself, I suddenly realized with a stab of pain that I was occupying the very same stall Holmes and I had shared the night of the Ramo Samyi performance.

Before I had time to do much more than reflect on the tricks of coincidence that a playful destiny visits upon we mortals, the curtained entry behind me opened again, and I heard a familiar nasal voice.

"Well, hallo, Dr. Watson, as I live and breathe. Fancy finding you in my box."

"Inspector Lestrade. What brings you here? I never knew you were an aficionado of the arts of prestidigitation and legerdemain."

"Hmmm. Yes. Well, I don't know about that so much. But, give me a magician every time. That's what I call good entertainment."

So saying, he sat down with a proprietary air, occupying the very seat which my dear departed friend had filled nearly two months ago.

"You see," he continued, "the Yard must necessarily be involved with a variety of continuing investigations. As a matter of fact, I am here at the specific request of M. Emile Houdin. He undoubtedly has learned that the disappearance of the magician's assistant, in which you and Mr. Holmes showed some interest two months or so ago, is one of our ongoing inquires. Because of his special invitation to me, it is quite possible that my presence was sought in an official as well as a social capacity."

As he possessively leaned back in his chair, lighting a cigar, I experienced a strong emotional resentment of this man. I was totally unable to reconcile this caricature of a detective with the memory of my confidant of many years, a genius of scientific deduction.

I glanced past Lestrade and observed movement in the semi-darkened loge across the well of the theatre.

"Look, Lestrade. Directly across the way is the giant hunchback Holmes and I saw the night the magician's assistant disappeared. In fact, that is the very box our mutual friend was examining the next afternoon when you came to tell us of the bombings at the Tower of London."

Lestrade glanced casually at the behemoth opposite us. "Yes, London does seem to attract more than its share of the miscreations of the world. But you know, Doctor, if a man who looked like that were a criminal, we would never have to worry about losing him. Since nobody could forget him, our problems in eyewitness identification would be over. But, things are never that simple, are they?" And he turned his attention back to the rapidly filling theatre.

Using my opera glasses, I randomly scanned the incoming, crowd and the occupants of the stalls and boxes around the parquet and horseshoe circles. I paused for a moment to take a closer look at the giant. He was huge! I estimated him to be nearly seven feet tall, and to weigh close to twenty stone. It was interesting to note that even seated, he continued to wear his red silk-lined, dark cloak clasped across his enormous chest.

The lights flickered and were turned low. All eyes centered on the proscenium. From the wings, a small Arabian lad appeared, rolling a kettledrum. He twirled the large padded drumsticks ceremoniously about his head, as the audience leaned forward in anticipation. He began a drum roll which rapidly increased in volume until it filled the theatre. As the crescendo reached its zenith, there was a blinding flash in the center of the stage. The tenuous smoke slowly wafted away, and as our sight returned, we saw the figure of Emile Houdin.

His father would have been proud. He spent the first hour of the performance enchanting and baffling his audience. He and his captivating assistant, Erin, turned a stuffed toy monkey into a live chimpanzee. She shot a loaded revolver at the conjurer and he caught the bullets in an apple. He caused Erin to be levitated, and made her disappear into thin air, only to reappear in a pumpkin. These and his many other feats of magic delighted and mystified his audience.

Finally, to thunderous applause, he walked to the foot lights and held up his hands for silence.

"Ladies and Gentlemen. I shall return shortly for the third act of this evening's presentation. Your programme calls attention to the appearance of your next performer, M. Host el Kebar. It is my extreme pleasure to introduce this renowned mystic for his very first appearance in Great Britain and Europe. He will now demonstrate for you acts of the supernatural from the mysterious Middle East. To my knowledge, he is the only man to leave his native country to come to Europe and share with you his unbelievable skill. He is not on tour, but this religious personage will exhibit as a favor to me, and as a treat to you, the mythical, often heard of, but never before seen, rope illusions of the holy men of Islam. Ladies and Gentlemen, M. Host el Kebar."

The small Arabian boy again started his drum roll, and as the sound pounded at our senses, another dazzling blaze of light obscured our vision. As it cleared, Emile Houdin was gone. In his place in the center of the stage stood a broad shouldered, tall, slender man. He wore crimson pointed slippers, wide baggy pantaloons, a short vest-like jacket secured at the waist by a brilliant red sash, and a matching turban with an emerald green stone set in the center. The generally light color of his garments accentuated his dark skin, and formed a perfect backdrop for his beak-like nose and sharp Middle Eastern features. He drew a wicked looking scimitar from his waistband, and extending his arm, held it parallel to the floor, cutting blade up. With his left hand he threw a green silk scarf high into the air, and allowed it to float down upon the motionless cutting edge. Its downward drift seemed totally unimpeded by the steel, the two pieces of the now cut silk floating uninterruptedly to the floor.

At this point the Arabian lad reentered, carrying a wicker basket, which he placed on the fakir's right. It was oval, unstained and about the height of a man's knee. The boy seated himself cross-legged on the stage with the basket between the two performers. He withdrew a bamboo flute from his belt and began playing an eerie melody with strange tonal qualities which were vaguely reminiscent of my service with the Fifth Northumberland Fusiliers in Afghanistan near its border with Persia.

Suddenly, the lid to the wicker basket was knocked aside, and, as we watched breathlessly, the end of a rope appeared and began to rise in the air. The fakir, who had been standing as motionless as a statue, now swung his scimitar over the top of the ascending hawser and completely around it, demonstrating that it was free of thread, string or other attachment. Meanwhile as the atonal strains continued, the rope kept climbing, higher and higher, and within two minutes, its upper end had disappeared into the visually impenetrable darkness above the stage. The bottom end was now completely out of the basket, and seemed to hover about a foot above the rim of the container.

El Kebar barked a command in a familiar sounding, but unknown tongue. The young boy began to tremble, as though in fear. Another stentorian order and the quivering youth sprang to the rope and began climbing hand over hand, as fast as he could. The fakir put his sword through the sash around his waist, and he, too, began scaling the slightly swaying hempen line in apparent pursuit of the young lad. At a height of about twelve feet above the floorboards, the boy disappeared into thin air, and within seconds thereafter the magician was likewise lost to sight.

I turned to Lestrade, saying, "They climbed incredibly swiftly, hand and foot on the right reaching upward, and alternating with the left hand and foot. Were it not for the presence of the rope, I would have described their movements as swimming upwards in the air."

Suppressing a full-throated shout, Lestrade exclaimed excitedly, "That's it! That's it! That's exactly the way the bomber disappeared after he had thrown the dynamite through the back window of Mr. Holmes' carriage."

His comments were interrupted by hair-raising screams of terror emanating from the area where the two performers had vanished. Suddenly, various members of a small human body began to rain downward onto the stage. Lestrade was frozen in shock. Members of the audience stood up in horror, and some even fled the theatre. Unexpectedly, the fakir rematerialized, descending the rope and holding his bloody sword in his right hand. As soon as his feet were again on the floor, the line collapsed and plunged downward into the basket. Quickly, el Kebar gathered all the gruesome remains of the boy, and threw them also into the wicker hamper. He then replaced the lid.

Again and again, he thrust his still dripping blade into the basket, as though he was trying to kill the lad anew. Some of the braver spectators moved into the aisles, and began slowly edging their ways toward the stage, crying, "Halt," "Stop," and other exclamations of protest.

Lestrade vaulted over the railing in front of the loge, shouting:

"That's murder, by God. You are under arrest."

Serenely, el Kebar turned to the house and bowed. He took one step backward, and raised both arms toward the sky. His posture was almost spiritual. His presence was so commanding that for just an instant, the theatre stilled, and the general forward surge of movement momentarily paused. In a soft and melodious voice, almost prayerfully, he spoke some strange, foreign incantation. As he lowered his arm, he made a half turn and threw his scimitar at the tympanum. His accurate throw caused the ivory handle to strike the drum head with a great booming sound. Instantaneously the top of the basket flew high in the air, and the grinning face of the Arabian boy appeared. Smiling broadly, he stood erect and stepped out of the basket, miraculously restored to life.

There was immediate pandemonium. Cheers of "Bravo," "Bravo," filled the theatre. And for several long minutes, M. Host el Kebar bowed and accepted the plaudits of the thoroughly mystified, thoroughly appreciative, but patently relieved, assembly.

When the ovation began to ebb. somewhat, M. Emile Houdin strode to the side of el Kebar and, after gaining the silence and attention of the hall, thanked his honored guest, highly praising his performance. In the middle of another round of acclaim by the wildly enthusiastic audience, there was yet a third explosion of light, and when we looked again, the stage was entirely bare.

I leaned over the railing to speak to Lestrade and to praise the incredible illusion we had just observed. But the Inspector at that moment could not have cared less about the artistry we had witnessed. His entire attention was focused upon the insight he felt he had gained during the performance of the Persian fakir. In fact he was now insisting that el Kebar and the boy were the culprits in Holmes' death, and he was, at least, by God, going to take them into custody for investigation.

"Dr. Watson," he said emphatically, "we are going to go backstage and arrest this fellow, el Kebar. He and that lad are the ones who threw the bomb into the hansom and killed Holmes. The boy who vanished from sight after that explosion swam upward in the air just as this Arabian youth did. Come with me."

As I stood up to leave our loge, I noticed for the first time that the opposite box, which had been occupied by the hunchbacked giant, was empty. In the confusion of the progressively terrifying illusion on stage, and the subsequent tribute to the fakir, I had not observed his departure.

Lestrade was slightly in advance of me as we hurried

behind the curtain.

The dressing room door was ajar, and Lestrade entered without breaking stride, pushing it all the way open. As I reached the threshold, I saw a mighty forearm in a choking hold across the throat of el Kebar, lifting the fakir completely off his feet.

The pressure which was being exerted must have been immense. His eyes began to protrude, and his skin was becoming even duskier in color. He was feebly pawing at the monster's arm with his left hand. With his right he reached downward and pulled a pearl-handled pistol from his bagging pantaloons.

I immediately recognized the firearm as the gun my departed friend had fired when he caught the bullet in his teeth at our Baker Street dwelling, nearly scaring me to death. I suddenly realized that Lestrade was entirely correct - that el Kebar was the murderer of my friend and colleague.

Lestrade drew his own gun, and leveled it at the giant at point-blank range. "Release that man, or I shall shoot," he ordered.

With his free hand the monster easily extracted the weapon from the magician's wobbly grasp, and, in a sudden upward and backhanded swipe, stunned Lestrade with a blow to the face. His legs buckling, the latter reeled backwards against the wall, obviously dazed and disoriented.

The giant took one step toward Lestrade, intending to disengage his firearm from his grasp, and I withdrew my blade from its position of concealment in my sword cane, a souvenir of my army days. During my posting to Afghanistan, I had taken the opportunity to visit Baghdad on a fifteen-day leave. In the markets there, I had found, and on a whim purchased, an ivory-headed, hollow metal walking stick, constructed to conceal a thin sword about twenty-four inches long. It became a rapier in the hands of its owner by holding the barrel of the implement firmly in the left hand, and twisting the handle briskly in a counterclockwise direction.

At this point I was quite prepared to sever the giant's hand to prevent him from taking possession of Lestrade's weapon. Apparently he understood my resolve, for at that point of time, but from what source I knew not, I heard a high-pitched childish voice shouting, "Away! Away!"

The titan shook the fakir as a terrier shakes a rat, and dropped him to the floor. He turned toward me. I was still blocking the door.

I looked high into the face of this monster. The chin was rounded and jutted out as far as an ordinary man's nose, the tip of which hung bulb-like over the fleshy lips. The eyebrows were unkempt and shaded the eyes to the extent that they were always shadowed from above, as the supraorbital ridge projected a half centimeter beyond the protruding frontal bones. The ear lobes which could be seen beneath the long hair were large, with thickened cartilage at the edges and hung pendulously almost to the level of his mouth. As his hand threw me aside, I noted the broadened and lengthened sausage-like fingers. The strength of this grotesque behemoth was such that in merely brushing me, I was thrown to the floor as he disappeared through the door and into the backstage.

In spite of the force of the backhanded blow which had knocked Lestrade into the wall, he had not lost his grip on his gun, and he was rapidly regaining his senses. He turned his revolver upon the fakir, whose eyes were starting to clear, and, in his best police manner, stated clearly: "M. Host el Kebar, I arrest you for the killing of Sherlock Holmes, and it is my duty to warn you that anything you say may be used against you."

The handprint of the giant still blanched the skin around the neck of the magician. Slowly the area began to turn pink as the circulation returned, but as yet he could not speak. He picked up a folded programme I had noted falling and swirling around the giant during the one-sided struggle. There was a fine precise script on it which seemed incongruous to the sausage-like fingers I had previously noted. The fakir thrust the paper at me, pointing to the writing.

I took it from his hands, and on the back I observed the following:

M. Host el Kebar

M HOST EL KEBAR

M H O S T E L K E B A R

B A R E K

BAKER

HOELMST   BAKER

HOELM   BAKER ST

HEOLMS

HOLMES   BAKER ST

The last line fairly jumped at me and I perceived that a child's game of anagrams had been played with the name of the performer.

I looked at the mystic more closely, and heard a weak rasping and croaking voice. "Yes, Watson, it is I."

I was dumbfounded. I turned to Lestrade, who was saying: "Drop that evidence. I'll see you stand in the dock for murder."

I saw that our often dull-witted friend still had not recognized the piercing eyes, the hawk-like nose, the aesthetic bearing, and the general demeanor of my friend and colleague whom I had believed had departed us forever. He was continuing his attempt to arrest the magician, still telling el Kebar - whom I now realized was Holmes - to put his hands up.

"It's Holmes, Lestrade. It's Holmes."

"What? What?"

At this point the mute Holmes peeled back his turban, revealing his sandy brown hair. He pointed to a carafe and tumbler resting on a makeup table nearby. I retrieved these items, and, with a shaking hand, poured a glass of water for him which he swallowed carefully. At this point his voice, though a little more than a whisper, returned.

"Quickly, we must follow that giant. There is no time now for explanations. He must not be allowed to escape."

We rushed through the narrow passageways behind the curtain, exiting by the stage door. We ran down the alley to the box office in the front of the theatre. "Have you seen a hunchbacked giant leaving?" I asked the ticket agent.

"Yes, governor. The rude lout neariwell trampled our doorman without so much as a by your leave."

"Which way did he go?"

"He took the first hansom in line, and I think that's it, just now turning the corner over there on the left."

We immediately engaged the next carriage in the queue with Holmes saying, "Quickly, driver, it is worth ten guineas to you if you can catch that cab."

The Warehouse

Whether it was Holmes' offer or a reckless streak in the cabby, I do not know, but the horse lurched forward and a break-neck chase ensued. We slowly started to gain on our prey. Perhaps the first driver was not as foolhardy as our own. But it was a ride to remember. When we started we were an estimated three or four hundred yards behind our quarry, and while we never made up all that distance, we certainly decreased their lead by half.

We turned several corners one after the other, and finally emerged into the Strand. From that point on, there was little chance of their escaping our pursuit. Fleet Street and Cannon Street passed under the flying hooves of our steed, and it was only after we had passed Gracechurch Street, executing an almost immediate right turn in the direction of London Bridge, that Holmes exclaimed, "He's heading for the docks."

Another series of abrupt turnings, and our villain pulled to a stop. We saw the figure of the giant exit his cab, and disappear into the gloom and darkness of what appeared to be an abandoned warehouse on the Thames. Thinking that the building had a rear entry, Holmes ordered Lestrade to circle the structure, and to prevent the giant from escaping by any means, including the use of his gun if necessary.

I followed him quietly into the interior with more than a little apprehension. Mentally I took stock of our weapons. Aside from Holmes' formidable intellect, we really had very little of an offensive or defensive arsenal against this monster. True, I was still in possession of my sword cane, and Lestrade had his gun. But, our adversary, in addition to his superhuman strength, was carrying Holmes' pearl-handled pistol. What my friend had in mind should we be fortunate, or possibly unfortunate enough to capture this colossus was as much obscured in shadow for me, as the interior of the warehouse was at the moment of our entry.

As anticipated, we were met with Stygian darkness. The only illumination of any kind came from the faintest glimmerings of the street gaslights outside, as they flickered through two dusty windows in the wall. We appeared to be in a small office or anteroom.

Holmes reached for my arm, and placing his other hand upon my shoulder, he brought his mouth close to my ear. "Careful, Watson, not a sound. I think we've tracked the bear to his cave and he is more familiar with it than are we."

As we moved slowly forward, my toe nudged something solid on the floor. With my right foot, I explored the base of the object, and when I was satisfied that it was inanimate and therefore would not attack me, I tentatively extended my hand. It appeared to be an empty wooden box of some sort. Picking it up, I carried it to one of the windows where the exterior street lamps seemed to provide at least a paucity of light. We could barely make out the faint markings on the container's exterior, 'Johnson Importers, ' plus the additional word,

'Explosives.' I started in shock and recognition. At that very moment, Holmes voiced his own identification in tones so low they would have been inaudible a few feet away.

"Aha, Watson. We have found the destination of the dynamite which was stolen from Johnson Importers, where the guard, Mr. Smith, was murdered. No doubt the bombs used at the Tower and upon my carriage have been assembled here. We must be doubly careful, as the parties for whom we search may yet possess some of the contents of that carton."

We slipped through a door which closed behind us with a barely audible click. We found ourselves in the cavernous interior of the warehouse proper. Vision was extremely limited. I could hear some faint sounds some distance away, but I could not define the direction of origin. We continued our deliberate and soundless advance.

Suddenly, up ahead, there was a spark of light which was resolved into a candle's flame. We edged closer. Dimly, we could see the giant unclasp and remove his cape, hanging it on the wall. The presence of other items of a man's wardrobe gave evidence that this place was used for habitation. He then backed up to a platform, the top of which reached approximately to his eighth thoracic vertebra. He fumbled at the front of his shirt for a few seconds, and then shrugged his massive shoulders, in turn, as though he were slipping braces from them. What followed caused my mouth to gape wide open! His hump - that abnormally large kyphotic mass on his back - was detaching itself from his body, and was settling down on the stand against which he stood.

We crept forward. The giant turned around, and began removing a covering from the deformity, inside of which there seemed to be movement. Unexpectedly, we heard a human voice speaking in an unusually high register - not unlike that which I had heard at the theatre within the last hour - just before the monster had knocked me to the floor in making his departure. The words, however, were indistinguishable.

Abruptly, there emerged from this 'hump' a small male figure, possibly three feet tall. He held out his arms to the giant to be lifted to the floor. For the first time we were able to understand his speech.

"God, it's bloody uncomfortable in there, but carrying me on your back all these hours is no fun for you either, my Ymir. But, first things first. Where are they - that meddlesome Holmes and his tiresome friend, Watson?"

At this point we were no more than fifty feet away from this oddly matched couple, the midget and the gargantuan. Holmes stepped from behind a mass of cartons.

"The busybody and his trusted friend are here in your lair, gentlemen, and outside to prevent your escape, should you try it, Scotland Yard awaits."

The dwarf gave out with a squeal of frustration and scuttled into the corner, while the giant calmly turned to face us. Peering past the monster, I observed the Lilliputian seize what appeared to be a length of thin cord hanging from the rafters, which he lit with a match. Immediately, there was a sputtering of sparks, and the odor of burning powder assailed our nostrils.

A fuse!!! That's what it was! A fuse!!! And undoubtedly connected to more of this deadly pair's dynamite supply, high in the overhead beams of the building.

As apprehensive as I was about this turn of events, I was comforted to hear the deliberate and unruffled voice of my friend.

"Good evening, good sirs," he said. "It is always reassuring for one in my line of endeavor to have his deductions confirmed, to know that certain conclusions one has reached are, in fact, true.

"I think it fair to state, my diminutive friend, that your passion for the Fenian movement greatly exceeds your physical stature. Your herculean efforts of the past months had made it obvious to me that I was seeking a malignant mentality. When it became manifest that your Ymir, with all his incredible strength, could not accomplish tasks which would require quite an undersized man, it was but a short step to conclude that your giant was, in fact, two men, one of whom had to be concealed in the hunch. One must look beyond the illusion and into the reality, no matter however improbable. For once you eliminate the impossible, the remainder, however improbable, is the truth.

"However, in point of fact, good sir, what you were attempting to do was so manifestly barbarous, and so utterly impossible, that it necessarily required the mind of an illusionist in order to eliminate the misdirection. An ordinary mind could not do this. And that is the reason why you had to get rid of me, because I was your greatest danger."

"My dear Mr. Holmes," the midget replied, "your existence is in more peril at this minute than ever before. That fuse leads to three pounds of dynamite, Mr. Nobel's latest contribution to humanity. Your utterly boring and absurd discourse has squandered fifty-five seconds of your rather limited life expectancy, which previously measured three minutes."

I took umbrage at this insolence to my close and dear colleague, and turning on the dwarf, I exclaimed: "Sir, how dare you! If you were twice as intelligent as you consider yourself to be, your mind, compared to the genius of a Sherlock Holmes, would give off but the light of a candle in the brightness of the noonday sun."

At this point, my friend turned to me, commenting, "Correction, Watson, a dying candle, flickering its last."

In the past both Holmes and I had deliberately provoked

adversaries, because, as Holmes was fond of noting, people make mistakes under moments of stress and provocation. The studied biting insult often may cloud a man's judgment.

Our undersized opponent, despite his formidable faculties, surrendered to his anger and emotions and began stammering. It was obvious that he was outraged and frustrated at not being given the recognition he felt his brilliance commanded, and which he craved from the superior intellect of a Sherlock Holmes. Recognizing his master's temporary loss of reason, the giant reached down and grasped the shoulder of the dwarf with one hand. With his other, he inserted two fingers through a brass loop in the floor, and lifted a sturdy trapdoor, leading to descending brick stairs. Gently pushing the gnome down the passage, he said, "Quickly, sire, to the boat. I will protect our rear."

Regaining control of his ire, the midget reassessed the situation. Appreciating that Ymir was right, he wasted no more time in idle repartee, and immediately descended the steps. With that, the giant, who had never looked larger nor more menacing, favored us with a deadly smile as he slowly retreated in the direction of his escape. I had my sword cane poised and I was determined to run the monster through if he made any motion toward us.

At the same time, however, the fuse was continuing to burn brightly as its sparks slowly spiraled upwards. An occasional gust from an open window high in the wall caused it to dance merrily to and fro like the tail on a kite. Seeking to give me an opportunity to cut the tether of that deadly firefly, Holmes, appearing very slight indeed, in contrast to the hulking figure of the colossus opposite, stood between me and our nemesis.

At the top of the stairway, the giant turned in our direction, and, from the pocket of his dress coat, in a very deliberate motion, he drew the pearl-handled firearm he had taken from Holmes at the theatre. He sighted along the weapon's barrel directly at the head of my friend. As I watched in horror, unable to move, he pulled the trigger, discharging the gun with a loud report.

From my left, unbelievably, I heard the imperturbable voice of my comrade.

"Watson, I'm in no danger from this buffoon," and he spat the bullet out of his mouth onto the floor, where it bounced in the direction of his assailant. Of course!!! This was the pistol which Holmes had used, when he had first demonstrated the illusion to me.

Ymir, however, was dumbfounded. He blanched, turned, and ran halfway down the steps exposed by the open hatch in the floor. As he reached to close the trapdoor, he gave us a parting venomous thrust:

"Perhaps you are impervious to bullets from your own gun, Mr. Holmes, but you and your doctor friend would suffer your throats being crushed and your necks easily snapped by my bare hands, a task I would hugely enjoy. It makes such a satisfying sound. Have you never heard it? A pity. But I must protect my master and flee from the coming explosion, and I must forego that pleasure.

"There is a time, my egotistical friend, when physical power has a greater advantage than brain power. You will find this to be true when you pit your mind and muscle against the weight of this trapdoor which I can move so very easily.

"The entry through which you passed, when you entered the caverns of this warehouse, is self-locking. You will find that it and this trapdoor are your only two means of egress. You will also learn that even together, both of you will not be able to raise this exit. There now remain to you but sixty seconds of life." He sneered, "Farewell, good sirs, indeed!"

With that he stepped further down the ladder and out of sight. The hatch door slammed closed with a clap of chilling finality.

"Quickly, Watson, from the platform, can you cut the fuse with the blade of your sword?"

A hasty glance told me that the use of the dwarf's stand was our only hope. Together we pushed the cumbersome base beneath the burning squib, and from its top I stretched and struck - in vain! It was simply too far beyond me.

"Holmes, I cannot reach it. Is there no other means of escape?"

Holmes ran to the trapdoor. "Assist me, Watson!"

The giant had been correct. Even with the adrenalin pumping, the two of us together were unable to lift the massive lid which the monster had handled so effortlessly.

My friend peered around the perimeter of light. "Watson, we have it!" He pounced upon a round iron bar about six feet long and approximately one inch in diameter. A solid block of wood about eight inches square was kicked in my direction.

"Someone once said that if one had a lever long enough, and a fulcrum high enough, one could move the earth. Let's see if our anonymous physicist was knowledgeable."

We inserted one end of our crowbar through the ring in the trapdoor, and we placed the block on the floor as close to the hatch opening as we dared. Exerting all our combined strengths, the door began to rise. As soon as its base was higher than the adjacent floor, I slid a piece of wood under it and we repositioned our pry. The second heave raised the door about a foot, and I braced it with an ironbound box. The third lift, and a second chest was placed on top of the first, and it was wide enough. In all candor, I must confess that had I been as slim as Holmes, we could have made our escape with the first carton alone. But my more corpulent figure made the second box an absolute necessity. As we reached the bottom of the stairs,

Holmes turned to me, and placing his hand on my shoulder, quipped, "My friend, neither strength nor intellect will prove your downfall; but someday you may fall prey to your girth."

The brick stairs we had descended led to a narrow foot walk several feet above the water. Ahead of us, we could see three small skiffs moored by davits set in the walls. The nearest was at least thirty feet away.

The entire passage was bricked with a rounded vaulted ceiling which was so low that we had to bend over as we ran. Our only illumination was the spirit lamp carried by the midget as he approached the furthest boat, and even that was partially obscured by the broad back of the monster as he hurried after his master, casting weirdly moving shadows in bright relief on the brick walls.

As our quarry reached the furthest boat, the dwarf jumped into the bow. Ymir grasped the docking rope and raced along the passage pulling the dinghy behind him. At the end of the walkway, he placed his hands on the transom and gave a final push, jumping into the stern and sending it out into the water. Simultaneously, the spirit lamp was extinguished as the gnome threw it far out into the river. In an instant we heard the powerful strokes of the oars as the giant maneuvered the craft from under the warehouse and out into the Thames.

My friend and I stumbled along in the darkness, and almost fell into another of the boats. Holmes swiftly loosened its ties, and with each of us on an oar, we rowed out of the tunnel, between the pilings supporting the loading platform. If Lestrade had followed Holmes' orders, he now stood above us, guarding the rear of the warehouse. Even though we were on our way to the safety of the river, instinctively we still were ducking our heads as the timbers of the pier were less than a foot over us.

Moonlight sparkled on the water before us, and I realized

we were nearly exposed to the forthcoming destruction. Holmes shouted at the top of his lungs.

"Lestrade, we are under the dock in a boat. Come to the river side, and we will take you aboard. " He accompanied his command with several sharp raps of his oar on the overhead beams.

Above us we heard Lestrade respond in typical Lestrade fashion.

"Hallo, what? Hallo, what was that?"

We pulled a few feet out from under the pier. Holmes stood up in the boat and roared, "Lestrade, there's a bomb in the warehouse. Jump!"

By now, Lestrade had spotted us. But still he just stood there. "What! What!"

Exasperated beyond comprehension at the man's obtuseness, I interrupted Holmes, and bellowed, "Lestrade, you bloody fool! The building's going to blow up at any second! Jump! Jump!!!"

He turned and looked at the warehouse in disbelief. After an agonizing second of hesitation, he spun around and began running toward the end of the quay. It is said that God watches over fools, and that night He had at least one eye upon Lestrade. The latter had taken no more than ten strides, when he tripped over a loose timber lying on the dock, and fell headlong into the river. For a brief instant, I saw him silhouetted against the sky, and we watched helplessly as we observed his service revolver fly from his hand and plunge into the Thames. One of our weapons was irretrievably lost!

We poled the boat to him and pulled him aboard. As we did so, we heard a tremendous explosion above and behind us, and the opposite bank of the river lit up in a brilliant flash. The detonation sent a shock of wind pressing our clothes against our backs.

Instinctively, we grasped the wharf's pilings and pulled ourselves back under its protective cover, ignoring for the moment the plight of our poor-inspector, floundering and gasping in the bottom of our craft like a fish brought to gaff. Burning timbers played a veritable tattoo on the pier over our heads, and we began to feel the heat of the flames.

Burned into our senses, however, at the time of seeing the initial blaze of light, was the shadowy outline of Ymir, rowing his boat rapidly down the river. Unfortunately, we could not give chase, as we had all we could handle in staying afloat in waves which threatened to swamp us and the falling timbers which bid fair to batter our brains.

When the aftermath of the destruction had subsided, and there was but a constant fire, we rowed out into the river. By this time, our villains had disappeared.

But, for all his misfortunes, Lestrade was not ready to give up.

"After them! After them!"

Holmes was silent for a moment "I fear it would be useless to follow at this time. With all that's happened, they now have nearly a fifteen-minute advantage on us. Our present situation demands intellectual thought, not a physical response. We shall return to Baker Street, as this appears to be a two-pipe problem. I anticipate, however, that we shall have a long journey ahead of us tonight once our destination is determined."

The Baker Street Irregular

Promptly upon our arrival at 221B Baker Street, Holmes placed a lighted candle in the window.

"Holmes," I exclaimed, "except for the three of us, all of London believes you were blown to bits nearly ten weeks ago. What makes you think there yet may be any Baker Street irregulars to answer your summons?"

"Watson, as much as I dislike to give public notice to the Fenians that I have survived the explosions in the cab and at the warehouse, our need for immediate assistance is greater than the danger that our lodgings are being watched. I fancy the irregulars are still extant, and on that subject we shall see. Be a good fellow, and ring down to Mrs. Hudson for some tea and cakes, while I build a fire for us."

We both busied ourselves with our respective tasks, and Holmes took it upon himself to locate a spare dressing gown for Lestrade. We laid our wet clothes before the fire to dry. Even before our landlady had sufficient time to prepare our tea, there was a sound on the stair followed by a sharp rap at the door.

Upon its being opened by Holmes, he confronted a short, freckled youngster, clad in a dirty jacket and knickers. His blond hair was carelessly tucked under a stained cap, and some of his toes peeked through rents in his shoes. The lad looked incredulously at my friend - as though he were seeing a ghost - but he said not a word.

"Ah, Wiggins, good lad," said Holmes. The boy nodded. "Enlist the aid of the irregulars, and post at least one to each of the railroad stations. The south side of the city particularly must be covered. You will be looking for a gigantic, hunchbacked man. It is possible that you will see a most unusually large man accompanied by a dwarf, but I am persuaded that the giant hunchback is the more likely. When you find him, observe what he does, where he goes, what train he takes from which platform, and report this information to me here. Now, go like the wind."

The street Arab touched his cap with the forefinger of his right hand, and turned and bolted down the stairs. As I watched from the front window, he raced to the center of the street, stopped, and putting his fingers in his mouth, he delivered several irregularly spaced ear-splitting whistles. He then took off on a dead run in the direction of Regent's Park.

"My dear Doctor, from the moment that candle was lighted until this instant precisely four minutes and forty-three seconds have elapsed. There is no further need to advertise our residency at this time. If you will extinguish the candle and draw the drape, we may continue our preparations for the evening."

I did as he asked, and as I turned around, we heard Mrs. Hudson's step ascending to our floor.

"Watson," Holmes said sharply, "I rather doubt that our

good landlady is quite ready for the shock of finding me alive and in one piece. Time enough for that later." And, as we heard her tap at the door, "Will you take the tray while I disappear once again - although temporarily, to be sure." With that he stepped into his bedroom and out of sight.

After our exertions of the previous hour, we made short work of the hot steaming tea, and, as always, a generous supply of cakes, cheese and biscuits provided by Mrs. Hudson. The biting chills and hunger assuaged, Holmes leaned back in his chair.

"Gentlemen," he began, "the problem before us is twofold. Our two friends very probably are holding captive two persons who have disappeared since this case had its genesis. We must proceed upon the assumption that both are still alive, although the present danger to them is probably exacerbated since their captors now know I am alive, and am on their trail. Second, it is quite obvious, if it were not before, that these blackguards who attempted to blow up the three of us at the warehouse, are affiliated with the Fenians. While this fact identifies them as enemies of the Crown, it may also serve to assist us in putting names and locations to them. I believe some of my reference materials will accomplish just that."

At this point, Lestrade interrupted. "Mr. Holmes, aren't you forgetting one thing? The Crown Jewels are a third part of our problem, as you call it."

"Lestrade, the jewels have never presented any great mystery. Their whereabouts are obvious to anyone who has the ability to look beyond the illusion and perceive the truth."

"Oh, come now, Mr. Holmes," said Lestrade with a patronizing smirk. "The Yard hasn't got a ruddy clue, and that's a fact. You can't expect me to believe that you've known where they have been all along. Do you take me for a bloody fool!!!"

"Nature is as nature does, Lestrade," said Holmes equably.

"The treasure is perfectly safe and can be produced at any time. There's no particular emergency about them. On the other hand, fancy that one, and probably two lives are in danger if we lose the scent we are now following."

"If what you say is true about two people being in jeopardy," Lestrade interjected, "then I should advise my superiors at the Yard, and perhaps they will send a squad of officers along tomorrow to be of assistance to you."

"My dear inspector," my friend replied, "there is insufficient time for that. We must depart as soon as our Baker Street irregular returns from his mission, and I fancy that will not be long delayed. Now that our adversaries know that they have me to deal with, I am convinced that if we cannot effect a rescue of the hostages within twelve hours, they shall be executed in the same manner as have all the others.

"No, Lestrade, cast your lot with us for the night, and I'll wager you'll earn a commendation from the Commissioner before we are through."

In his response, Holmes, of course, had made a psychological appeal to the venal side of Lestrade's nature. The latter was not above accepting credit for an achievement which was primarily the result of another's effort, and he no doubt recalled that on more than one occasion in the past, the hierarchy of command at the Yard had singled him out for praise when the major portion of the endeavor had been that of Sherlock Holmes. One could almost see the succession of conflicting emotions chasing each other across his brow as he weighed his decision. But, as with so many men, cupidity won, and, muttering to himself, our good inspector withdrew to a chair near the fire.

Holmes looked up. "Watson, will you be kind enough to retrieve my scrapbooks and my books of heraldry. Ah, splendid, thank you." Whereupon, my friend lit his malodorous pipe and began to peruse the materials I had delivered into his possession.

As his second assault upon the contents of the Persian slipper drew to a close, I was roused from my dozing by his exclamation.

"Gentlemen, the game is afoot. We must get our coats and prepare to depart. Our Baker Street irregular is even now on his way up the stair. Our pursuit will lead us first to Victoria Station. Watson, bring your sword cane, and I shall arm myself with the American derringer."

His words were no sooner out of his mouth and there was a pounding on the door, which I promptly opened. Wiggins burst in, out of breath as though he had run a long way, and between lung-filling gulps of air, blurted, "Mr. Holmes... Cartwright... saw a giant hunchback... at London Bridge Station... The hunchback... stole a handcar... He left on track four."

"Good work, lad, good work, indeed. And the same to Cartwright and to all the irregulars Quickly now, hail us a hansom for Victoria. Off with you."

Then, to us, "We must make haste. Victoria's track three intersects track four from London Bridge south of Sydenham. Lestrade, we'll need to commandeer a handcar at Victoria to give chase, because the next train doesn't leave for nearly three hours. By leaving London Bridge with a handcar, that blasted dwarf has stolen a sixty-five minute jump on us."

When we reached the street, Wiggins had a four-wheeled hansom waiting, and, as we climbed aboard, Holmes shouted to the cabbie, "Victoria Station, my good man, and with all possible speed."

Our ride was the second to remember that night. Our driver must have been a fugitive from Ascot. He took 'all possible speed' quite literally, and we hung on for dear life. Even as we were careening wildly through the streets and avenues of the city, Holmes, with a hanger strap in each hand, raised his voice to a near shout.

"Gentlemen, in spite of the noise and the imminence of our being pitched out of our seats, I must acquaint you with our situation.

"A good many years ago, the Queen conferred knighthood upon Sir Alexander Hyde, a captain of industry, shipbuilding to be precise, and a large landowner. Sir Alec had two sons. For reasons of their own, perhaps because they felt their father was exploiting Irish immigrant labor at the shipyards, perhaps because the family had many of its roots in Ireland, both sons became active in the Irish Home Rule movement. Louis, the younger of the two, and really a very nice chap, for all that anyone knows, has been most active in the Gaelic League, which, as you may or may not know, was founded by a Trinity College Professor, Eoin MacNeill, and his son. The older of the Hyde siblings is Jonathon, and he is the midget who made his appearance from the giant's hump at the warehouse. He succeeded to his baronetcy upon the death of his father some four years ago. He has been, and is, most active in the Fenians, and undoubtedly bears primary responsibility in the bombing of the Tower of London.

"Baron Jonathon has extensive holdings in Ireland, some near Galway and some close to Cork. But he also inherited a small property near Earlswood, about twenty-five miles south of London. It is a smallish castle, built in the late 1200s or early 1300s, and now reputedly in serious disrepair. However, it would serve admirably as a temporary holding camp for outlaw Fenians, until the necessary arrangements could be made for getting them out of the country."

"I say, Holmes," I inquired, "when did you first become aware that our villains were a midget and a giant?"

"Ah, my friend, there were several indications from which the careful observer could deduce that we were certainly dealing with more than one person.

"First, Watson, recall our visit to the Egyptian Hall Theatre the night the magician's assistant disappeared. You will remember that the loge directly opposite ours was occupied by a giant hunchback. When I examined that box the following afternoon, I found traces of Turkish cigarette ash on the carpet. Our friend, the giant, did not smoke that night.

"Second, my magnifying glass detected scuff marks in the carpet below a chair that for all that was visible to us that evening was unoccupied. Those scuff marks were such as might be made by a young lad whose legs were just barely long enough for his feet to reach the floor.

"Third, my lens also enabled me to perceive child-size footprints on the floor of the basement, and similar hand prints in a very light coating of dust on the cage-like box located against the wall on the four-wheeled cart.

"Fourth, there were two noticeable flickers in the flame of the lamp providing illumination to the giant's box. This would indicate that someone left and returned to that loge during the performance of Ramo Samyi. That sequence was not visible to us. Our line of sight would have permitted us to observe anyone who was tall enough to be seen above the top of the velvet in front of the loge. That height is forty-two inches above the level of the floor.

"Fifth, Watson, is your own experience in the theatre basement. When the folded programme was taken in the darkness, it should have told you that your mysterious caller was of very light weight, smaller than Wiggins. Even a very slender framed adult could never have crossed that floor, moving alternately from rug to planking, without making some sort of boot or surface noise, and yet you heard nothing.

And, my dear friend, while you may not hear yourself snore when you sleep, I am quite aware that, when awake, you have excellent hearing.

"Of course, our experiences tonight at the theatre and at the warehouse confirm that Baron Jonathon is not only the hunch on the giant's back, but the brains behind these often bizarre acts of violence and terror as well."

Throughout this recital our driver had been true to Holmes' admonition of 'all possible speed.' Our steeds had been running as though they were being trained for the Derby, and between the twin responsibilities of hanging on and attending to my friend's explanations, our abilities had been taxed severely. On several occasions our natural body inertia nearly cost us our seats, as the horses were pulled up sharply from time to time to avoid foolhardy pedestrians attempting to cross our route.

A Pumping Pursuit

In spite of our harrowing ride, we arrived at Victoria Station in one piece and little the worse for wear. Holmes tossed the cabbie a guinea as a reward for his speedy, if precipitous, trip. Lestrade, using the badge of his office, commandeered a handcar for us, and, with the assistance of two of the yardmen, we set out on track three in pursuit of our quarry.

Without any specific direction from anyone, Lestrade and I took the first turn in providing the pumping operations necessary for our manual trolley. Holmes was crouched at the very front of our transport, facing into a slight breeze and providing a forward lookout. The weather was cool, but not uncomfortably so, and the sky was partially overcast.

"I say, Mr. Holmes," Lestrade said suddenly after a few minutes. "This is risky business. We could run square into an incoming train, or be overtaken by one for that matter, and then where would we be? The Yard doesn't know where we are. Nobody knows where we are, and if we get hit, there won't be enough left of any of us to tell anyone what we're on to."

Without turning around, Holmes replied, "Lestrade, it may have escaped your attention, but Watson knows that long ago, I committed to memory the timetables for every inbound and outbound train from and to every London station. I can assure you that barring any specials, we are perfectly safe. In fact, our warehouse malefactors, by leaving from London Bridge, have exposed themselves to more inbound traffic than we shall encounter. It is for this reason, of course, that we are departing from Victoria.

"In any event, we shall have ample warning of the approach of any danger to our persons, and between the three of us, I rather imagine we could remove our self-propelled carriage from the tracks with time to spare. When we get to Sydenham, anything inbound and ahead of us would have to get by Baron Jonathon and the giant first. But in view of Ymir's prodigious strength, I hardly expect a London bound express to assist us in their capture by disabling them for us.

"By the way, Watson, do you have any familiarity with Norse mythology? No? Then the name of the midget 's tame monster - Ymir - means nothing to you. Ymir was the Scandinavian giant from whose body the gods created the world. Aptly named, I'd say, except this chap wants to destroy this blessed land we know."

In this manner we continued our journey. Lestrade and I settled into a comfortable rhythm and we began to make good time. There was very little conversation, and our passage was nearly silent, except for the clicking of the wheels as the rails rolled by beneath us. When I became winded, Holmes relieved me on the pumper, and I assumed the job of lookout. When my respiratory rate returned to normal, I exchanged places with Lestrade, who in turn traded with Holmes after some moments of rest. In this fashion we continued the chase. We passed noiselessly through the stations at Brixton, Herne Hill,

West Dulwich and Sydenham Hill. Shortly after leaving the latter behind, Holmes spoke quietly.

"We must be alert now. The junction with London Bridge is approaching rapidly, and I will have to throw the switch at that point so that we may change tracks."

We slowed our pace somewhat and within a matter of a few minutes, Holmes called for us to stop. He jumped off the cart, and I was right behind him. We ran perhaps twenty feet to the junction switch, which we threw to permit our passage to the London Bridge line. Again Lestrade halted the handcar for a moment to allow us to reset the rails. And, with all three of us again on the platform of our vehicle, we resumed the chase, alternating, as before, with our turns on the pumping bars.

The half-moon peeped from behind the clouds at intermittent times in the partially overcast sky. It was during one such period of brief illumination, about twenty minutes after we had switched tracks, that Holmes, acting as lookout at the time, spied the silhouette of the car bearing the two scoundrels we were pursuing. In a low voice, he advised us that the midget was sitting at the front of their trolley, his back to the wind and facing us. A moment later we could make out the hulking figure of the giant pushing and pulling down and up in a strong and even rhythm.

Suddenly, Ymir dramatically increased his tempo, bending his back with a will, and, even though Lestrade and I responded as best we could, the giant slowly began to pull away. There was little doubt that we had been spotted. Now the chase began in earnest.

Our ally, the moon, elected this moment to play hide and seek with the cloud cover. For minutes at a time, we were unable to see their cart or their activities aboard it.

Suddenly, from the platform ahead, we saw a small flare of light, which resolved itself into a reddish glow, ascribing an arc ascending perhaps ten feet in the air and then falling to the ground. As we drew a little closer, but still about one hundred twenty feet away, we could see the sputtering of a fuse between the tracks ahead.

"Those bloody bastards," shouted Lestrade. "That's dynamite!" Straightening from his pumping labors, he jumped off the cart, his centrifugal force sending him tumbling down the slight grade beside the rails.

Personally, I confess to a moment of terror. "It's going to blow us up! Stop!! Stop!!!"

Without a word, Holmes reached down and calmly applied the hand brake, locking the wheels Amid a shower of trailing sparks, we screeched to a stop a little less than one hundred feet from the burning fuse. Simultaneously, Holmes and I leaped from the cart and threw ourselves prone upon the ground, covering our heads with our hands. Within two or three seconds a deafening roar, accompanied by a shuddering of the earth, announced anew the detonation of Mr. Nobel's invention. For several seconds we endured a deluge of rocks and debris.

As soon as it appeared safe to do so, we regained our feet, brushed ourselves off, and walked forward to inspect the damage. There was a saucer-shaped hole in the roadbed perhaps ten feet in diameter. One of the rails was completely severed, and the other was twisted tortuously. It was obvious that the section was totally impassable, and that the handcar would have to be lifted across the pockmarked portion.

At this point we heard a hoarse cry from the general area in which Lestrade had abandoned ship. "Hallo! Anybody hurt? Mr. Holmes, Dr. Watson, are you all right?"

Holmes responded with more than a touch of asperity in his voice.

"Lestrade, you blithering buffoon. Get yourself up here.

This handcar will have to be carried about thirty feet across this bomb crater. We need your brawn at this moment."

Holmes and I returned to our vehicle, just as Lestrade staggered into view. Hatless, dirty and begrimed, he was a sorry sight. The knee of one of his trouser legs was torn, and one sleeve was nearly severed from his jacket. He was noticeably limping, and blood was trickling from one knee, a hand and his right cheek. I made a quick inspection of his wounds and determined that none were serious. With a bit of soap and water and the liberal application of some strong astringent, our inspector, except for some sprains and abrasions, would be good as new.

Between the three of us, we struggled and muscled the handcar across the explosion area and placed it on the undamaged track. After a moment to collect our respective breaths, Holmes, as usual, returned to the problem at hand.

"Gentlemen, this manifestly presents a grave hazard to rail traffic upon this line. I estimate that another fifteen minutes will see us into Merstham, where we must stop and inform the stationmaster to telegraph the appropriate warnings. In the meantime, Lestrade, let me have your undershirt and greatcoat. We must post a warning. Although I am quite certain we shall arrive in Merstham in ample time to give appropriate admonitions of the perils to be found here, we must not chance an assumption that further attempts to delay us will not be made."

Although he was slightly bewildered by my friend's somewhat peremptory demand, Lestrade removed and handed over the designated items of apparel. Swiftly and dexterously, Holmes fashioned them into something resembling a human figure, using Lestrade's somewhat grey undershirt as the head. He draped the crude mannequin across the twisted rail. From a distance and in poor light, it indeed did give the appearance of a human body on the track. This tactic recalled to my mind his use of a bust of himself in the window at Baker Street for the capture of Colonel Sebastian Moran, and I again marveled at his use of an illusion to create an effect.

By this time we were again probably ten minutes behind our villains. True to his estimate, it took us a trifle over fifteen minutes of hard and exhausting pumping before we arrived at the Merstham station. We suffered a further delay in explaining to the stationmaster the condition of the track over which we had journeyed and the hazard it presented. I was somewhat at a loss to understand our difficulty in communicating this fact to Mr. Allen, as that was his name. He appeared to be in a highly agitated state. But Holmes was equal to the task of persuading him to compose himself. That accomplished, we learned that a giant and a midget about ten minutes earlier had arrived in the same fashion as ourselves. They had paid him handsomely for the only available horse and carriage in the immediate vicinity, and had disappeared at breakneck speed in the direction of Redhill.

Holmes consulted his legendary memory for transportation and geography.

"Let us push on to Redhill ourselves," he said. "The Baron's castle is northwest of Earlswood and southwest of Redhill. We can try for public conveyance there, and we should have slightly less distance to cover."

Thus it was that the three of us found ourselves back in our hand-powered chariot, pumping hard, and changing the lookout periodically, as one would relieve another.

About twenty-five minutes later, we pulled into Redhill. While it was not the end of the rail line, it was about the limit of our endurance. With aching backs and shoulders, we climbed off our handcar stiffly, puffing deeply.

Our stationmaster here, Mr. Steven, confirmed the fact that the Merstham agent, Mr. Allen, had indeed telegraphed the necessary warning about the track being cut. Repair crews were even now on the way.

I heated some water on the stove in the station and washed Lestrade's wounds. At my request, Mr. Steven rummaged through one of the railway company's boxes and, finally, triumphantly produced a small bottle of disinfectant which I applied. We were now ready to continue our chase.

Assault on the Castle

Transport was to prove another problem. There were no public stables in the nearby town. So, Lestrade, over the strenuous objections of Mr. Steven, and for the second time that night, was forced to use his authority to appropriate what was available, the stationmaster's private donkey cart. The incident served to demonstrate that on occasion the blustery of Lestrade could accomplish an end which could have been attained in no other way. While it made one cringe at times, his braying, bully-like arrogance simply brooked no further argument.

True to the ways of its genre, the beast was reluctant to say the least. With the three of us occupying the cart, he refused to move at all. We made the early discovery, however, that if one of us would walk ahead of him, he would follow. That lesson learned, Holmes strode off in a northwesterly direction, while the inspector and I rode in the wagon. Since Holmes had told us that the dwarf's castle was about seven miles distant, we knew we had an almost two-hour journey before us, and that meant we should be arriving in the early dawn.

We took turns leading the donkey, with Holmes calling the directions when we encountered an intersection. Our pace, while by no means speedy, was steady.

Perhaps thirty minutes before sunrise, but with the dawn's light providing fair forward visibility, Holmes, again in the vanguard of our forces, raised his hand in the manner of a military commander who signals halt to his troops. He pointed toward the crest of a small hill before us. Through the rising mists of the early morning, we could make out the stone remnants of what once had been a Norman castle. Much was in ruins, but there were recognizable portions that still stood in various stages of disrepair. The most intact structure was the keep which towered over all other sections.

"I believe from this point," said Holmes, "we should approach on foot, and as silently as possible, although it is most unlikely that we shall long remain unobserved."

We slipped the harness from the donkey, and pulled the cart into some low brush at the side of the path we had been following. Lestrade found a length of rope, a part of the animal's harness, and with this we tethered our Biblical beast, which Holmes in some flight of pixyish whimsy had named Gomorrah. (Even unto this date, I am still awaiting his explanation of how or why he came to fasten such a sobriquet on that unfortunate quadruped.)

This accomplished, we moved forward as quietly as we could, taking advantage of such cover as the terrain provided. We could see that there was a moat to be crossed. The outer curtain of the castle was mostly in ruins, and I judged it to be nearly three hundred feet along its sides. It appeared that once we were across the moat, we would experience little difficulty in negotiating the rubble. The portcullis at the gate was raised.

The inner curtain was in a much better state of repair, although there were areas where time had reduced its integrity. I was certain that we would experience a minimum of difficulty in finding some means of breaching this secondary wall, and thus gain the inner ward.

When we reached the moat, we were cheered to find it to be dry. Time and the elements had eroded the steep sides, and this once formidable line of defense was now little more than a ditch about six feet deep. The slope of the banks made our crossing simple.

We clambered over the irregular stone blocks and fragments of the outer curtain, and, while we were engaged in this advance, I noticed irregular wisps of smoke escaping from the upper regions of the keep. I pointed out this indicia of habitation to my friend. He stopped and studied the phenomena for several seconds.

"Well, Watson, someone is certainly in residence. The use of fire opens several interesting avenues of deliberation. It is, of course, an appropriate time for breakfast. We should also bear in mind that since this castle dates from the 13th century, the original occupants repelled invaders by pouring boiling oil from the battlements. Alternately, we can be sure that Baron Jonathon has an escape plan for use in the event that he cannot eliminate us, and the employment of hotly charged air as part of a design for flight leads to even more interesting speculations."

Our movement across the rocky debris of the outer wall was without incident, except for a single slip by Lestrade which ended with his getting his left extremity caught in the stones. It took my assistance to free his boot, and, except for a few scrapes on his shin, he was none the worse for wear.

We thus arrived in the outer ward without indication that we had been observed by the castle's occupants. We paused and listened intently for any sounds from our opponents which might give us a clue to their location. We heard nothing but the breeze in the brush and the calling of the morning birds. Immediately, we began our search for a means of ingress to continue our penetration of the castle's defenses.

After completing nearly a full circuit of the inner curtain, we found a likely portal in the wall opposite the pastern gatehouse. The ravages of the centuries had completely rusted through the upper hinge, and it was but child' s play to force our admittance. Except for the smoke from the keep, which looked a little heavier now, there still had been no sign of the dwarf or the giant.

We found ourselves in a disused corridor which led to what appeared to be the barracks for the castle's garrison of soldiers, and it was here that we found our first evidence of habitation. Embers in a large stone fireplace were smoking slightly, and various pots and utensils manifested their recent use by what appeared to be a residual coating of some sort of greasy stew, still soft to the touch. A few tattered blankets and skins on the floor gave testimony that this area of the castle had boasted occupants quite recently.

Holmes stirred up the ashes, peered into the kettles at hand, and turned over the threadbare remnants with his foot. A few beetles and spiders scuttled for cover.

"Soldiers, Holmes?" I asked.

"More likely outlaw Fenians, I think, Watson," he replied, "who have evacuated, I deduce, within the last two hours. On their way to Ireland, I suspect."

"Not in hiding out there, waiting to attack us then?"

"No, Watson, they've cleaned out. There' s nothing left behind that a man would return for. One always knows when a place where men have been living has been abandoned. There is a complete absence of the day-to-day implements and accouterments, however primitive, with which modern man surrounds himself. There is none of that here. They are gone."

Holmes posted Lestrade as a sentry at the door to the inner ward, an area probably close to one hundred fifty feet wide and about an equal distance in length. In its exact center was the keep. Once upon a time, the inner ward had evidently been filled with the then-current thatch roofed huts for the full-time residents of the castle. Here and there one could see foundations for such dwellings, but otherwise nearly all traces of what must have been a flourishing community nearly five or six centuries ago had virtually ceased to exist.

My friend and I sat down on some stones in the old barracks next to Lestrade for a moment's rest. I wanted to know what was next in store for us.

"What do we do first, Holmes?"

"With the probable exception of our two rogues, it is apparent that the place is uninhabited," he began. "If there were any defensive forces on the premises, our progress to this point would have been severely contested. As it is, our arrival here in the inner ward with no deterrent structures between us and the keep, leads me to the conclusion that we have only the two of them to deal with.

"Let us assume, however, Watson, that there are two other residents of this antiquated pile of stone. Let us assume, further, that they are no threat to us, but rather have been placed under restraint, because they are prisoners of our quarry. Now, if those two captives were Guri, the assistant of Ramo Samyi, and the party in whose interest you had a short, but distinguished, career as a personal emissary of the Prime Minister, then, my question to you, sir..."

"My God, Holmes," I interrupted, "are you saying these people have Prince Edward here? In this castle?"

Before my friend could reply, we heard the sound of a person gasping as though being strangled. Lestrade was looking at us in utter incredulity, his eyes wide open and his mouth agape. Under different circumstances I should have laughed aloud. But I realized immediately that Lestrade had never been privy to the fact that the Prince had been kidnapped. Inwardly, I cursed my careless tongue.

"No matter, Watson," said Holmes, as if reading my thoughts. "This would have been made known to Lestrade within the next two hours in any event. But, back to my question. If you were Baron Jonathon, knowing that your sole defense was Ymir, to whom would you afford greater protection, Guri or the Prince?"

"Why, the answer is self-evident, Holmes," I responded. "Prince Edward, of course. He is far more valuable - as a bargaining weapon, if nothing else!"

"Splendid, Watson. It is thus logical to deduce that Guri within the last hour has become of no further use to Jonathon. Therefore, it is probable that she has been abandoned, somewhere here in the fortress."

With this, he bounded to his feet and strode through the door into the yard of the inner ward. He paused, and starting on his left, he intently studied the structure's walls overlooking the area in which we were standing.

"The three most logical places to find our captives, on the one hand, and to confront the enemy, on the other, are the castle's prison, the royal apartments, and the keep. If Prince Edward is to be the bait for an exchange, he must be close at hand to Jonathon, and it is most unlikely that the baron would confine himself to the dungeons just to be near His Royal Highness, but that is the most likely location to find Guri. Hence, we should visit them first. In a garrison of this vintage, I believe they were often built below the barracks."

As we hurried through the soldier 's quarters, heading to the passageway by which we had entered, Lestrade, having found his voice, excitedly kept trying to interrupt and query Holmes about the Royal kidnapping, but my friend would have none of it. To whatever it was that the inspector would say, the response was always the same.

"Not now, Lestrade. Time enough for that later. Right now, speed is the essential."

We came upon a stairway, which had entirely escaped my attention upon our entry. As it was under cover and constructed of stone, it was in fairly good repair, and we experienced no difficulty in its descent. At the bottom we found ourselves in a large basement or storeroom with nothing to suggest that it had ever had use as a prison. There was a well in one corner, which still appeared to be in operating order. In fact, as Holmes and I peered into its depths, we could hear the sound of running water. At that precise second, we heard a faint undulating wail, as though some animal, somewhere, had just suffered a mortal wound. The sound brought a chill to my spine. Holmes, however, was galvanized into action.

"Lestrade, Watson, quickly! There is an open valve in the well! It is draining into something beneath our feet. We must gain access to whatever is under this floor! Someone's life may depend on it!!"

The light in the basement was meager enough, but fortunately what openings to the exterior there were happened to be on the east side of the inner curtain, and this fortuitous circumstance provided us with probably the best light of the day.

Within minutes Lestrade had found a section of floor timbers which were not pegged into the underlying joists. Feverishly, the three of us threw the roughhewn lengths aside. As soon as it was wide enough, Holmes cast himself onto his hands and knees, with his head and shoulders thrust far down into the opening. Just as abruptly, he raised his head, and without saying a word, but in great haste, seized my cane, withdrew the sword, and with a single slash cut the ferrule from the base of the stick.

As he had withdrawn from the now open hatch, I had looked in. To my horror, I saw the face and upper torso of a young girl almost completely immersed in a tank of steadily rising water. Her head was tilted back as far as possible, and only her face was above the roiling Niagara. Holmes thrust the now-hollow stem of the sword cane toward her mouth.

"Watson, hold her nose! She must be made to breathe through her mouth!" Reaching as far down as I could, I did as he asked. The girl's eyes, verging on the brink of madness, seemed to clear a little. I noted that her arms seemed to be down at her sides, as though tied. Holmes had seen the same thing.

"Lestrade, the lass is bound to something; either on the tank or at its bottom. This is no time for modesty. Shed your knickers and get her out of there."

To Lestrade's credit, he did not argue. Even though he must have known that the water was icy cold, and that he would have to submerge his entire body while locating and freeing the restraints, he made no protest, and he moved with dispatch.

From a position sitting on the floor, he dropped into the tank. We could see the top of his head, as his hands followed the captive's arms downward, searching for her bonds. In a few moments, he broke the surface, and, gasping and gulping for air, exclaimed:

"Her wrists are tied to stones on the bottom and I can't move them. I need something to cut the lines."

Without a word Holmes handed him the blade from the cane, as I continued to grasp the girl's nostrils. Lestrade disappeared from view again, but when he came up this time, one of her arms was locked tightly around his neck. Holmes had been holding the hollow walking stick, and now, leaning even further into the opening, he used his other hand to deliberately and gently disengage Lestrade's back and shoulders from the frantic grasp of the terrified young woman. Thus freed, Lestrade, after another couple of lung filling gulps of air, again sank below the swirling waters in search of the other wrist. It seemed that an eternity passed, but our man from Scotland Yard would not be denied. When he finally emerged from the depths of the tank, he brought the girl with him. It was Lestrade's finest hour.

Holmes and I carried her up the staircase to the rooms of the barracks, with a teeth-chattering, shivering detective-inspector right behind us. Holmes' observant eye had recorded the presence of a fireplace there. While he and Lestrade gathered all the flammable materials they could find, I examined our wet and critically chilled prize. Although she was nearly unconscious from the cold, I was satisfied that her only probable sequelae were ones associated with prolonged exposure to near freezing water. As soon as the fire was going, I put her before the blazing timbers, turning her slowly, much like meat on a spit. I wanted all surfaces of her body to feel the heat of the flames. I laid my head on her chest, and heard no sounds of fluid in her lungs.

Thus reassured, Lestrade was selected to stay with her, while my friend and I again took up the chase. They were both wet, and she was in no condition to accompany us. On the other hand, it would have been folly to leave her without some protection. Holmes handed over the derringer with instructions to promptly shoot the giant if he appeared in the doorway. I admonished Lestrade to keep our lady as warm as possible, and to get her moving on her feet, back and forth in front of the fire, as soon as she was able to do so.

"Watson," Holmes announced, "in spite of the fact that some of our smoke is going to be visible to our friends, we must resume our pursuit. I think our next area of exploration should be the apartments on the upper floor. While we now have one of the persons we expected to find here, the other's whereabouts is still a mystery. Further, I need not remind you that our two villains have not yet revealed their respective presences."

The Clash of Giants

We crossed the outer ward to the gatehouse of the inner curtain. It was there that we expected to find a staircase leading to the royal apartments. We ascended as quietly as possible. The living quarters of the centuries' long-departed owners, and their immediate retainers, occupied the entire west side of the interior structure, and were perhaps one hundred fifty feet in length.

We slipped through the southernmost portal of this section into a long, open corridor overlooking the courtyard which surrounds the keep. Once there had been a stone balustrade about thirty-six inches high on the right side. It, too, had suffered the ravages of time and inattention. In some areas the elements had so taken their toll that only the rudimentary foundations upon which the pilasters had been set remained. On the left of the passage, however, were numerous entries leading into what I assumed to be the usual living chambers.

We stepped through the first door and found ourselves in a

large hall. A fireplace occupied its south end. Corbels high on the walls bore witness to the locations for the lamps utilized by the long-departed inhabitants. There were vestiges of plaster here and there, and some massive oak beams had fallen on the quarried floors. Off to the left there were three smaller cubicles, which I took to be the bedrooms. Obviously, this was one of the apartments, but it did not have the more decorative appointments one would expect for the lord and lady of this 13th century fortress. Centuries of neglect had piled debris everywhere, and the continual erosion of time, wind and rain had washed away some of the mortar. Many of the stones had crumbled or shifted, and in certain areas the structure was highly unstable.

As noiselessly as we could, we worked our way in a general northerly direction down the open and windy hallway, peering into each room as we passed. Toward the end of the passageway, we came upon what seemed to be an extraordinary accumulation of rubble. Beyond these piles of stone and weathered timbers, however, our corridor was virtually clear, even though the balustrade was largely nonexistent. Holmes looked carefully at this large volume of litter, and laying his right forefinger vertically against his mouth in the universal gesture of silence, we retreated several paces, and stepped into one of the vacant side chambers.

"Watson," he whispered, "there is far too much rubbish in the hallway ahead of us to have been caused by the natural erosion of the corridor alone. In fact, the vertical and overhead structures are in better repair at this point than in some of the areas through which we have already passed. Now, my good friend, what does that suggest to you?"

I pondered his question for a moment, and replied, "It tells me that someone has chosen that particular locale as a place to stockpile the ruins from certain areas of the castle which have been cleared."

"Excellent, Watson. I absolutely agree. Then, what better conclusion can we draw than that this debris has been withdrawn from the next apartment and from the passageway in front of it? Why? Because those are the quarters Baron Jonathon and his Ymir have chosen to occupy while they are in residence. We must be exceedingly cautious as we approach, as one or both of them may even now be on the premises."

Returning to the corridor, we began our advance as stealthily as any soldier seeking to employ the tactic of surprise in his approach upon an enemy post. As we neared the last entry, we could hear sounds of movement from within, as though some heavy object were being dragged across an uneven floor. Grasping the sword from my cane firmly, Holmes leaped across the threshold. I was right on his heels. For a space of approximately two seconds, we framed the entry, each of us on opposite sides of the doorframe. Across the room, and perhaps twenty-five feet away, Ymir was crouched over a large iron strongbox. A quick glance to my right and left told me that we had not yet caught up with Prince Edward or Baron Jonathon.

A deep, unintelligible cry of fury burst from the throat of the monster. Seizing the chest by both hands, he straightened up and exercising all his inhuman strength, hurled it directly at my friend. Holmes must have anticipated such a stratagem. He stepped nimbly to one side, allowing the coffer to crash with a clap of thunder into the stone wall behind him. The force of the impact shattered the lock on the box, and its contents of gold and gems spilled over the floor. The glance of a second's time told me there was a fortune in the jewels alone. The entire end of the building shuddered.

In retrospect, it was here that the giant made his fatal mistake. Had he made a rush for the door, or for either of us, while his treasure-trove was still in the air, he might have made his escape. During its trajectory our attention was momentarily diverted, and before we could have reacted he would have had the advantage of several steps. Instead, he had waited to observe if his missile would find its mark, and verbally to vent his spleen.

"Now I have you, you meddling fools. Now you will suffer the power of Ymir' s hands. Now you will hear the snap of your own spine when I have the pleasure of breaking your necks. For all the trouble you have caused my master, now you will die in agony."

For a second, his threats hung in the air. Then, tossing an eye in my direction, Holmes shouted:

"Watson, on your left!"

Two strides brought me to the fireplace, above which was mounted the spiked mace of a 13th century warrior. I wrenched it free, and turned to find the monster advancing on Holmes. He was in a semi-crouch, his widely spaced feet shuffling in half-steps toward my friend.

Holmes began to circle to his right, away from me, holding his sword at the ready. Immediately, I divined his strategy. He wanted to position himself on the other side of the room, so that Ymir could not have both of us in his vision at the same time. If he had Holmes in his sight, he could not see me, and vice versa.

"Watson, guard the door." The command was unmistakable.

I returned to the entry, ready on Holmes' order to mount an attack. In a matter of seconds, the giant saw what my friend was doing, and, reacting to our placements, he paused and then began a slow retreat to the wall behind him. He made alternate half-lunges at each of us, growling deep in his chest. But whether he moved in my direction, or towards Holmes, the mastery of the blade developed over the years by my friend kept him at bay. Riposte and parry; riposte and parry; always with that deadly Sheffield steel flashing within inches of his face or throat.

"Well, Watson, once again we meet this buffoon - Mother Nature's joke on the human race."

Instantly, I understood my friend's tactics and I knew what was expected of me. We would bully, insult and belittle this monster, thereby provoking him into a rage in order to disrupt his capacities of reasoning. We had exercised this ploy on many occasions. Indeed, we had done the same thing to the master of this very giant.

"Yes, Holmes," I replied "It is provocative indeed. In the daylight, he is even more ugly and more misshapen than I noted last evening. It will be interesting to see how he reacts to just the two of us. After all, he is off Jonathon 's leash, and there is no one around to tell him what to do or say."

"Yes, well, I'm afraid we can't expect too much, Watson. Doing some act that demanded some slight intelligence might give him some human characteristics. One has only to look at him - painful though that may be - to know that this wretch has a long way to go before he becomes cretinous."

Then, addressing Ymir directly, Holmes continued:

"You misbegotten ape! In that fatty cranial mass some poor benighted scientist might call your brain, you haven't even begun to realize that you can't get out of this room unless you kill us both. And that you cannot do, because, if you attack one of us, at that moment you will perish by the hand of the other."

Our contrived verbal diatribe was having its effect. Ymir had attempted to drown out our verbal assault upon him with screams of anger, liberally sprinkled with vulgarities. Now, the sounds emanating from his chest were more animal-like than human. He was literally shaking with rage. Flecks of foam appeared at the corners of his mouth.

He apparently made the decision to deal with me first in his attempt to gain the hallway outside. Suddenly, and without warning, from eighteen feet away, he rushed. He could move astonishingly swiftly for so huge a man. His long, powerful arms were outstretched toward my throat. I swung the mace from my heels. His left hand caught the staff of my weapon, snatching it from my grasp. Just as his enormous right hand reached for my eyes and face, the spiked ball of the mace, swinging on its chain in a whipping motion from the centrifugal force of my pivot and turn, caught him hard in the upper left ribs. He gave out with a loud grunt, and dropped to his right knee. He put the knuckles of his right hand on the floor as he scrambled for balance. He gave every indication of his intention to continue the battle.

As he regained his feet, albeit somewhat unsteadily, he made a half turn and started for Holmes. From across the room, I saw Holmes' right hand and arm flash forward. The sword made a lazy quarter revolution in the air, and buried itself in the right shoulder of our assailant.

The giant staggered. He tried in vain to reach the still quivering blade with his left hand, and his feeble gropings in that direction made me realize that the blow of the spiked mace had undoubtedly splintered several ribs. There was no way a colossus of even his strength and unquestioned courage could overcome the incredibly excruciating pain on his left side. At that moment, both my friend and I were weaponless, and if Ymir had had the use of even one arm, it might well have been the end of both of us. I am sure it was for that reason Holmes placed the blade as he did.

As it was, the giant looked from one of us to the other, as he stood swaying in the center of the room. In that flash of time, he looked more like a great wounded animal than a human being. Finally, fixing his eyes on the door, he lurched from the chamber. Turning left along the passage way, he stumbled and tottered his way toward a descending staircase at the north end of the royal apartments. Holmes and I stepped just outside the entry to watch his progress.

"Holmes, he is on the way to warn the baron, who is truly the evil one in this piece. Shouldn't we stop him somehow?"

Laying a restraining hand on my arm, Holmes replied quietly, "No, Watson, the beast is sorely wounded and no threat to us now. Let him go."

Almost before the words were out of his mouth, the monster staggered and bounced off the left wall of the corridor. He reeled drunkenly to his right attempting to regain his balance. As he did so, his right foot tripped over one of the base stones of the rubble of the wrecked balustrade, and he started to fall. Without the use of either arm to save himself, the consequence was inevitable. His right hip struck the edge of what remained of the eroded parapet, and his momentum did the rest. Almost majestically, he rolled over the edge and fell without a sound onto a pile of rocks in the courtyard nearly twenty-five feet below. The side of his skull hit the surface with a dull, crushing sound.

Holmes and I rushed down the stairs to where he lay. It was unnecessary to make even a cursory examination. He was quite dead. His neck was bent at an acutely abnormal angle, and his left parietal region was pulpy in the area of its first contact with the stone.

"Look here, Watson," said Holmes musingly. I walked around the body. He pointed to the giant's throat. His weight and the force of his impact apparently had disturbed the equilibrium of the mass. In the shifting of the heap that followed, a large triangular stone had been dislodged, and, following the immutable law of gravity, it had toppled downward, striking the dead man in the neck.

"His throat is crushed," I said in a tone of near awe.

"You must admit, Watson, the presence here of more than a little poetic justice. Two magician's assistants, the royal cabinetmaker and his daughter, two guards - all have died at the hands of this man. All have had their throats crushed. Whitworth and Johnson had their necks broken as well. The fact that the immediate cause of death here was the splintering of his skull on these stones does not diminish the enormity of the irony of the broken neck and crushed throat of their murderer. What a holiday the boys of Fleet Street will have. If we borrow the style of our friends at the bar, the headline would read: CRUSHER NOW A DEAD CRUSHEE.

"I say, Holmes," I began. "Your placement of that sword was masterly. He had snatched the mace from my hands in spite of my best grip on it. Then, even crippled as he was in his left arm and side, he still would have been more than a match for me. I am again in your debt, sir, as have I been so many times in the past."

Holmes looked gravely at me for a moment. Then, with a sympathetic wrinkle around his eyes, he responded. "I must repeat what I've said before. I'd be lost without my Boswell." He paused for several seconds. "But, my friend and biographer, Baron Jonathon is still very much alive, and free to work his malevolent mischief. And, I'll wager you a farthing or two, he still has the Queen's son as his prisoner. Come, let us explore the keep."

Flight

Because our attention for the past thirty or forty minutes had been devoted exclusively to our search of the royal apartments, and on our battle with the lately departed Ymir, we had not given much heed to the keep, although earlier we had seen smoke emanating from its top. Now, as we craned our necks upward, we saw what appeared to be a large grey ball sitting on the battlements of the tower. I confess to an initial first impression of an ominous mushroom pileus.

"A hot air balloon, Watson!!! It's a hot air balloon, and it looks close to launch! Haste, Man, haste!!!"

We pounded up the keep throwing stealth to the winds. There was not a second to be lost! Holmes kept urging more and more speed, but I simply could not move any faster. Even then I stumbled a few times, catching myself with my hands on the stone steps in front of me.

About what I judged to be halfway up, we began to hear the roaring of the fire as it heated the air trapped inside the balloon. The sound increased in volume as we ascended higher, and the knowledge of what it meant kept us driving upward on legs of lead. I willed myself to keep going long after I had run out of strength and breath.

At last we burst through the flat door on the roof and into the bright sunlight. The envelope was gargantuan. As Holmes pushed the hatch to one side, I glimpsed an object rolling into the corner. A second glance identified a burning fuse and two red colored sticks, taped together.

DYNAMITE!!!

The next few seconds were a blur of activity. Although this scrivener will probably require several pages in the recounting of the events that followed, for the most part the total time involved hardly exceeded twenty ticks of the clock.

Holmes and I both rushed for the gondola. There was a silhouette of an absolutely motionless man standing on its far side. From the interior of the platform, I saw the midget cut the tether rope and the balloon leaped free. At that precise instant, Holmes' body was actually in the air as he hurdled over the side of the basket. I attempted to follow my friend, but my exhausted and trembling legs failed me. Just in time I seized a cable, affixed at its upper end to the bottom of the gondola, and at its lower to a millstone. I later learned that such a device is fairly common among lighter-than-air enthusiasts. Its purpose is to reduce oscillation of the balloon and basket, much the same as the tail on a kite.

Thus it was that I was carried aloft, clutching a trailing length of hemp and standing on a centuries old implement used by the castle's residents for grinding grain. I revolved slowly at the end of this following line, and found that another passenger was also enjoying the flight at the end of a rope, and at about the same distance beneath our aerostatic platform as I. This was the statue-like person I had glimpsed on the roof when we had erupted on the scene.

But there, any similarity ended. My aerial companion was bound and gagged, and the line which secured him to our wind-blown vehicle hung from over the side of the gondola in which I could hear Holmes and the dwarf in heated argument. I looked and looked again. There was no mistaking that familiar face. Trussed like a chicken though he might be, he still managed to convey a certain air of aristocratic, even insouciant, bearing.

"Prince Edward, I believe," said I, bowing cautiously, while maintaining a death grip on my umbilical cord.

My neighbor blinked his eyes in acknowledgment, and inclined his head slightly in my direction. He then raised his eyes overhead and I followed suit.

Holmes' right hip was perched on the edge of the basket's rim, one foot swinging lazily. Directly opposite him stood the object of the Prince's attention, Baron Jonathon Hyde. The latter's right hand was holding a knife, its blade just inches from the hempen line supporting the bound figure of the next in line to the throne of England.

Except for the soft sighing of the wind in the rigging of the balloon, our passage was soundless. The voices of the two men above us were clear and distinct.

"Mr. Holmes," the baron was saying, "I know you are an honorable man. I am prepared to reveal the whereabouts of the Crown Jewels if you will guarantee my safety out of England."

"Your Lordship, your proposal suggests to me that you are a sporting man. May I offer an alternate proposition, the content of which includes both subjects embraced in your undertaking?"

"State your bargain, Mr. Holmes."

"Thank you. My investigation of the disappearance of the

Crown Jewels has led me to draw certain conclusions as to their present venue. On that premise, I offer the following: I will disclose my deduction as to their location. Now, first, if I am correct, you will become my prisoner. Alternatively..."

BOOM!!!

A crash of thunderous proportions shattered the silence. The concussion rocked the balloon and gondola wildly, and we heard shards of stone screaming through the air in close proximity to us. In fact, one splinter of rock struck a metal chest on board the basket. Holmes picked it up idly.

My friend had been interrupted by an explosion behind us. At once, I recalled the burning dynamite we had encountered when we reached the roof. I turned and looked back. Nearly the entire upper half of the keep had been destroyed. Even as I watched in fascinated horror, whole sections of the granite walls, deprived of lateral support, fell away, crashing atop the roofs of other castle structures or to the ground. My God, we had left Lestrade and Guri in the barracks, and my eyes told me that a large measure of the rubble from the detonation had fallen upon that section of the fortress.

Could the Fates be that cruel!! Were all our efforts to find, and then to save, that lovely girl to have been for naught! It would be tragic enough to lose Lestrade, even though at times he vexed us sorely. But as an officer of the law, he was expected to lay his life on the line should the occasion demand. But Guri - now to be denied her future just when she was to be freed and reunited with her husband!! Tears for the futility of it all blinded my eyes, and I suppressed an involuntary cry of agony.

When I had myself under better control, I looked upward toward the occupants of the basket. The dwarf was bent over the side with all of his attention riveted on the destruction he had wrought, an evil smile playing over his countenance. Holmes was to his left, and positioned so that he could keep one eye on the ground, and the other on our foe.

Suddenly, I saw Holmes lean over the vertical rim of the gondola. He cupped his hands around his mouth and roared, "Lestrade!" For a moment I thought that he, too, was voicing his grief over the senseless barbarity perpetrated by the diminutive fiend above. Abruptly, he extended his arm, forefinger pointed to the ground in the general direction of the southern entry to the castle. I turned my attention again to the area being indicated, and I spotted two figures - one male and the other female - emerging from the dry moat.

"Lestrade!"

"Guri!"

Holmes and I shouted the names simultaneously. In response the two people on the ground looked up and waved.

Instantly, all the dismay, all the frustration, all the heartbreak of the past few seconds were swept away to be replaced by an intoxicating exhilaration, heightened, I am sure, by the depth of the depression I had just experienced. They were alive! And though we were leaving them behind, Lestrade could get the girl into Redhill by way of the donkey cart, and from thence to London.

For a moment, total silence reigned. I saw the gnome shrug his shoulders, as he turned his attention back to my friend.

"Ah, yes, Mr. Holmes. You were in the process of offering me the other side of a bargain. If you can tell me the site of the Crown Jewels - which I doubt - I am to become your prisoner. You were about to favor me with your alternative. If your conclusion is in error, sir, what then?"

"Then I will guarantee your safety out of England," Holmes replied.

The man opposite me shook his head violently at my friend's response. Like his Mother, the Prince, too, was made of stern stuff.

"But," Holmes continued, "there is one condition which is not negotiable to either, or both, of the terms of my proposal."

"And that is?" the dwarf interrupted.

"That Prince Edward and Dr. Watson are immediately to be pulled aboard this overgrown flower basket in which we are riding. That must be clearly understood."

"Mr. Holmes, I am prepared to deal with only one matter at a time. You cannot possibly know where the jewels are secreted. So, my fine detective, your bluff is called. Tell me where they are."

"Right where they have been ever since the moment of the explosion at Wakefield Tower, Baron Jonathon. In the false bottom of the display cabinet in the Jewel Room at the Tower of London. A false bottom constructed to your order by a royal cabinetmaker, half out of his mind with fear for the safety of his daughter whom you held hostage. And when the job was done, in return for his cooperation, you ordered their deaths at the hands of your tame monster, and consigned their bodies to the Thames. And now, my traitorous lordship, you will kindly put down that knife. By the terms of our agreement, you are my prisoner."

Upon hearing these words, the midget screamed in fury, stamping his feet in a child-like tantrum on the floor of the gondola.

"Curse you, Sherlock Holmes! You tricked me," he cried. "I made no such agreement! You won't win that easily!"

So saying, he slid the knife he held in his right hand under the rope, at the end of which the Prince of Wales was tethered, and in a low tremulous tone of voice, almost as if he wanted to weep, he began his tirade:

"You are a devil, Sherlock Holmes! Because of you,

everything has gone wrong. Two days ago, the Fenian garrison here at the castle was ordered to break camp and to proceed to another station at thirty past four o'clock this morning, an hour before Ymir and I arrived. If they had been here, you would be dead by now.

"Had you been two minutes later in gaining the keep, this balloon would have been launched, and your precious Prince and I would have been gone. My agents brought him here from Ireland the day before yesterday, and had you not interfered, I would have dropped his body on the doorsteps of Buckingham Palace as a lesson to the English government."

His voice was steadily gathering in volume, and as he continued, strong overtones of hysteria became apparent.

"But you haven't won yet. Unless you promise to get me out of the country, I'll cut this line, and the blood of the English tyrants will be upon your head. I'll consign him to the same hell he and his family have made for the poor people of Ireland! I'll never be your prisoner!"

The dwarf's vow was scarcely out of his mouth, when Holmes' long right arm whipped forward, and we heard a screech of pain mingled with rage and frustration. The knife flew from his hand in a high arc, and, turning end over end, disappeared toward the ground below.

The midget was staring unbelievingly at his right hand, shaking his numbed fingers. Droplets of blood stained his shoes and clothing. Holmes had thrown the splintered shard of stone, which, minutes before, he had aimlessly retrieved from the basket's floor, striking the dwarf's forearm. Our Fenian fanatic was now disarmed. All the color drained from his face, and he looked frantically from side to side, for all the world like a frightened animal.

"Baron Jonathon Hyde," intoned my friend in the coldest tone of voice I had ever heard him use, "thus endeth the siege of terror which you have waged against the Crown and the people of England. You shall be delivered to the legally constituted authority of this country. I have no doubt you shall be imprisoned in the very tower you so recently sought to destroy. I will give evidence against you in six murders, numerous attempted homicides, including my own, two kidnappings, a number of counts of sedition, and one charge for willfully destroying property of the Crown. I will not sit as your jury, but I have little doubt that you will be convicted, executed and your estate forfeit.

"Now, sir, for these purposes and for the safety of the rest of us, I must place you in modest restraint. As an honorable man, I give you my word that I will make your bonds as comfortable for you as I can, consistent with your security."

"But, wait, Mr. Holmes, wait! You do not understand!" protested our villain. "My actions against Prince Edward, against you and against those other unfortunate people have been justified by the laws of England to which you have always fully subscribed!

"Baron Jonathon, you are presuming to tell me that cold-blooded murder, political kidnapping for ransom, and sedition against the Crown are sanctioned by the laws of England? You are mad, sir!"

"What I did, Mr. Holmes, was only to act in self-defense - in self-defense of the persecuted Irish, fighting for their lives against the English oppressors. When I ordered the killings of those magician's aides, the two elderly guards, and the cabinetmaker and his daughter, when at my direction Prince Edward was taken prisoner and transported to Ireland for a time, when I attempted to accomplish your death by bombing - all of these were for the sole and only purpose of defending the right of the Irish to live as an independent people, free from the unlawful interference of the English swine. You were all casualties of war - nothing more. God chose me as His instrument in this battle, and doing His will is not a crime. I am guilty of nothing!"

Without comment, Holmes picked up a length of wire and began a measured approach upon the midget. His movement apparently broke whatever catatonic spell the latter had been under ever since he had lost his knife. Like a crab, he scuttled backwards into the farthest corner of the gondola. Further retreat was impossible.

Without saying another word, Holmes continued his relentless advance. It must have been the appearance of that implacable figure, for suddenly the dwarf grasped the lines of the rigging of the balloon and started to climb. It was at once apparent that he had little trust in his benumbed right hand. Using his left extremity freely, he was forced to employ his right wrist in his 'hand over wrist' ascent, as Holmes later described it. He continued upwards, almost halfway up the side of the balloon, where he stopped, breathing heavily.

Holmes made no attempt to follow him, although he continued to watch his scramble from the gondola. Once it appeared that Baron Jonathon was going to stay where he was, my friend's attention was turned to his passengers below the basket.

After studying the problem for a few moments, Holmes called to us:

"Your Highness, Dr. Watson must come up first, because he can be of assistance in bringing you aboard. Therefore, if you will just bear with us for a few more minutes, we'll soon get you out of your present state."

He picked up a length of stout manila cord about three fourths of an inch in diameter. One end he secured to a cleat on the gondola. He then set about fashioning a series of knots about eighteen inches apart, tightening and testing each one. Throwing the knotted rope over the side, he began to swing it back and forth in my direction. As soon as it came close enough for me to grasp, I caught it in my left hand. Holding both lines as tightly as I could, I placed my feet on one of the convenient tie nodes, and released the one connected to the millstone. After several seconds of heart stopping undulations and rotations, which added a few grey hairs to my head, I steadied and began a cautious climb to the basket. Holmes called encouragement, glancing overhead from time to time at his unrestrained prisoner. When I reached the platform, my friend lent his manual assistance and soon I was standing inside the gondola gulping great draughts of air in relief. After entirely too brief a time given me for recovery, we turned our attention to the Prince. Since he was bound tightly, we could expect no assistance from him. It was to be a lift of dead weight, dependent on sheer muscle power. With a few pauses along the way to rest and catch our breath, we hauled him up, and, I'm afraid, ignominiously manhandled him over the side. It was hardly the way royalty was customarily piped aboard a vessel.

My pocketknife with the three-inch blade finally severed his bonds, and he could at last speak and move about. Only then did Holmes and I observe the barest amenities due the future King of England. Again, and for the second time that morning, I put my medical education and training to use in the performance of a perfunctory physical examination. I concluded that except for some emaciation and malnutrition, due to forced inactivity and improper diet, the Prince was in satisfactory health.

He thanked us graciously for finding him and freeing him from his confinement. Turning to my friend, he asked: "What do we do now, Mr. Holmes?"

"The winds this morning appear to be almost directly out of the south, Your Grace, and they should take us straight to London. I estimate that our altitude is around six hundred feet, and that we are being carried along at something less than ten miles an hour. Certainly, we are going to have to put down at some point or other, but as long as we keep this course, I would suggest that we simply ride along. If current conditions continue, we should be over the city in two to three hours." Then, raising his voice slightly and looking upwards toward our passenger, he continued, "Perhaps we can put down at Buckingham Palace. After all, the Crown, a generation ago, was the source of Baron Jonathon's title, and a visit to Buckingham would be a return of sorts for our friend up there in the rigging."

As might have been expected, this sally provoked a stream of invectives from on high which the three of us chose to ignore.

"But, Holmes," I ventured, "how do you know this wind blown contraption will stay in the air for those two hours or more if we elect to continue this flight? Will we not lose buoyancy as the air in the sac cools?"

"Ah, good questions, Watson," replied my friend. "However, you will observe these pockets all around the rim of our basket. Those pouches contain lead weights to act as ballast, which we can throw overboard to increase the buoyancy you speak of in order to prolong flight. Additionally, the higher the sun rises as the morning wears on, the less heat will be lost from the balloon because of the rise in the atmospheric temperature. Thus I really do anticipate that we can ride the vagaries of the winds for the next several hours.

"But to consider another subject for the moment, I suddenly find that with all of the exertions of last night and this morning, I am ravenously hungry. I'll wager the baron, gourmand that he is, has some food and drink stored in one or more compartments of this flying platform. Let's have a look, shall we?"

In a very few minutes Prince Edward found the dwarf's cache, and happily we divided some cold pheasant, bread, fruit, cheese and sweets among us. There was even a bottle of French wine, which the Prince pronounced excellent. We invited Baron Jonathon to join us, but his only response was to mutter a few obscenities, and climb a little higher.

The Inevitable Hour

After our little repast, there was time to relax. One of us, on a rotating basis, was assigned to keep the watch. We were willing to continue the balloon ride as long as our course remained in the direction of the city. The other two kept an occasional eye on our captive, engaged in some desultory conversation, and even dozed briefly.

It was during one such period that Holmes, addressing a question to Prince Edward, brought me out of my reverie.

"Your Grace, perhaps you would be good enough to recount for me the circumstances of your abduction."

"There really isn't a great deal to relate, Mr. Holmes," he replied. "After the Ramo Samyi performance at the Egyptian Hall Theatre, the six of us in my party went along to the Criterion for a light supper and champagne, after which we all parted. I instructed my coachman to proceed to my companion's residence, and after I had seen her safely inside her dwelling, I returned to my carriage, intending to return to Buckingham Palace. When I entered the vehicle, someone - I know not who - pressed a rag soaked in chloroform over my mouth and nostrils, and I have no recollection of anything further until the following day, when I awoke in the basement of some farmhouse, tied up like a pig ready for the pit.

"Two weeks later I was smuggled out of the country into Ireland, where I remained until two days ago, at which time I was returned to this place. And, Mr. Holmes, that is really all I can tell you."

"I suggest you were brought here by the messengers who carried the orders for the Fenian garrison to break camp at thirty past the hour of four this morning," Holmes observed thoughtfully. "Baron Jonathon has already advised us that he had rather dramatic plans for you."

Thus we passed the next one and a half hours. We had no wagers to be won, no speed records to challenge. Our only interest in the longevity of our flight was that it carry us somewhere near the center of London. It was a pleasant, relaxing interlude, welcome in its release from the tensions and dangers of the past eighteen hours.

As we crossed the outskirts of the metropolis, it became possible to begin to identify some of the more prominent features of the central city. The morning air was clear and almost balmy, and, as we drifted along, we could hear the sound of the birds. Occasionally, we were the recipient of a wave and a shouted salutation from the ground.

"Your Grace," Holmes chuckled, "two hours or so ago, I facetiously commented that if the wind held, we could set down at Buckingham Palace. Of course, that was uttered in jest, because that would be asking a lot of even an experienced ballooner. But, now, I seriously believe that that vast expanse of green about a mile dead ahead is St. James Park, and with a judicious handling of the air valves and the ballast, we very probably could put this bag of hot air somewhere within its borders."

"That would be most appreciated, Mr. Holmes," the Prince replied in a similarly jocular vein. "I should enjoy a short stroll to inform Mother that her son is yet among the living. I must tell her to abandon her plans for changing the succession to the throne."

Smiling, my friend continued his cautious and skillful bleeding of the superheated air from the air bag, causing us to lose altitude very gradually. As we descended, our forward speed slowed as well. Holmes estimated that we were down to about four hundred feet, and our ground speed to be a little less than five miles an hour.

Our passenger aloft, early in the voyage, had attempted to demonstrate his bravado, hurling imprecations and threats from 'on high,' as I once commented. As time passed, he had become more quiet, although we had heard him muttering to himself from time to time. Now, he suddenly called down.

"I say, Prince Edward. When we land, are you going to be the proper English gentleman and give me the same sporting chance you would give the fox or a wild boar?"

The three of us ignored him. As soon as it became apparent that he was to get no response, he continued. "You cannot treat me like a common criminal! I have a title! Your Mother awarded it to my Father. At the very worst, I should be placed under house restraint until I can be deported."

For a moment, Prince Edward reacted not at all to this outrageous appeal Then, slowly, he raised his head and addressed the dwarf directly.

"Your analogy to the hunt for a wild boar or a fox is specious. English monarchs for centuries have exercised their right to confer knighthood on deserving commoners, and Queen Victoria very properly recognized the contributions made by your parent in the service of my country. But the Crown is also cognizant of the fact that a titled descendant may be far less worthy than his honored ancestor. Peerage once bestowed continues until the courts of our land have formally decreed that the lineal progeny have committed sedition. That judgment accords to the Crown the authority to strip the title from the traitor and declare his lands forfeit. No, Baron Jonathon, you will be imprisoned in the very tower you attempted to destroy, and there you shall remain until the charges against you have been disposed of - by your being found not guilty, or by execution of your sentence."

Screaming wildly, the midget uttered a terrible oath and shook his fist at us. "You'll never get me in the dock! Neither you, your Mother Queen, Sherlock Holmes, nor all of Scotland Yard! You'll never hold me - never in a thousand years!!!"

The area below us now was well populated, and we were attracting more and more attention. At one point we passed directly through the steam and smoke of a locomotive pulling its cars outbound from Waterloo Station. The ascending heat from the engine pushed our balloon appreciably higher, and we emerged into the sunlight again with traces of soot on our clothing and exposed flesh. Holmes released some more air from the envelope, and we resumed our continual descent.

Holmes called me to his side. "Watson," he said, "we shall be down shortly, and it is imperative that our passenger aloft be taken into custody immediately. Be good enough, if you will, to keep a sharp eye out for a mounted Metropolitan policeman, so that we may apprise him of his duties."

I posted myself on the opposite side of the basket. I noted with some surprise that we had captured the interest of a bevy of people who were running through the street apace with us. It seems to be one of the laws of our civilization that a collection of transitory human beings inevitably will draw attention from the constituted legal authorities. Shortly, I saw on my left an officer on horseback, moving to intercept the crowd.

When he was close enough to hail, Holmes relinquished his hold on the air-release valve for a moment. He rimmed his mouth with his hands and shouted.

"Hallo, Constable," pointing at the man with his index finger extended. "Can you hear me?"

It is doubtful that the policeman had full comprehension of my friend's inquiry, but he had seen and heard enough to know that he was the object of our attention. He reined in his stead, and plainly cupped his right ear.

"My name is Sherlock Holmes. With me is His Royal Highness, Edward, Prince of Wales. We have a prisoner who is to be charged with murder and treason. I am going to attempt to land this balloon in St. James Park. Gather some assistance in order that you may make him your prisoner when we put down."

Unquestionably, the man understood. He brought his right hand up to his visor in a salute. His horse wheeled around and set off at a full canter ahead of our path of travel. He glanced over his shoulder from time to time to check our line of flight, blowing his police whistle nearly constantly.

Within three hundred yards, he was joined by three other mounted officers. There was much gesticulating in our direction, and, as we swept overhead, they kept pace with us as nearly below our gondola as the streets and buildings of the city would permit.

We were much lower now and Holmes bled more air from the envelope. I judged that we were now less than two hundred feet above the ground and moving forward at no more than two or three miles an hour.

Using the points of the compass for reference, with North being our line of flight, and the front of the balloon,

I was standing about 300°. Holmes was on the east side, manipulating the air-release line, and Prince Edward was in the very bow of our airborne vessel. The three of us were intent on the panorama slowly unwinding beneath us, and to this day I have no idea what caused me, suddenly apprehensive, to look upward.

The dwarf had moved! From a position on the left side, approximately halfway up the sac, he had worked his way downward and toward the front of the balloon to a point about twelve feet above the rim of the gondola. Incongruously, a part of my mind registered the fact that he was still using his bent right wrist to grasp the ropes of the rigging. He was almost directly above the head and shoulders of Prince Edward who was leaning forward over the basket's side as he watched the scene below.

I could see in a flash that the traitorous baron was going to make one last desperate assault on the hated English Crown. Just as he released his hold and dropped, drawing up his knees so that in addition to the momentum of his fall, he could add the force of a kick to the back of the unprotected neck of Prince Edward, I lunged! There was no time for ceremony and less for a warning. Without so much as a 'by your leave, sire,' I body-checked the future King of England as vigorously and as proficiently as befitted an old rugby player of the Blackheath football club, whose demands of excellence I remember to this day.

The Prince lost his battle to retain his balance, staggering and skidding in Holmes' direction along the railing of the gondola. The dwarf's right knee hit me in the area of the left scapula with a jarring impact, and he fell heavily to the platform. The force of the collision spun me, counterclockwise, toward Holmes and the Prince. For a split second, all action ceased, the audacity of the attack having surprised us all. Crouching on the far side, our murderous baron confronted us, and, across a distance of ten feet, the three of us looked at him.

He was the first to move, and the momentary hypnotic spell which had immobilized all of us was broken.

As our adversary leaped to the top of a locker which was lashed to the far side of the gondola, Holmes and I dove headlong for the madman. And here, like his Ymir, the baron committed his mortal error. He hesitated! With his feet about thirty inches above the top of the basket's rim, he stopped momentarily to physically vent his vitriolic spleen one more time. Snarling like an animal, he kicked at us. In a reflex of pure self-defense, I caught his ankle. Regrettably, my left-handed grip, already partially numbed in receiving the brunt of his attempt to kick Prince Edward over the side, was unequal to the task. He wrenched his foot free from my clutching fingers as he scrambled upwards in his attempt to escape.

In his panic, he forgot or disregarded the limited function of his own previously wounded right hand. His climb, from the underside of the balloon, was upwards and outwards on the lower quadrant of the west side. Gravity made him totally dependent on the strength and agility of all four of his extremities. His right hand had no strength, and in his haste he failed to compensate for that loss, neglecting to use his wrist on that side.

The rope of the rigging slipped from his grasp, and, clawing frantically at the air, he fell away. I grabbed for him wildly, but even though his clothing brushed my hand as he plummeted past, there was no saving him. His primal scream of utter horror followed him all the way to the sickening thud of his body upon the stones of the parade ground over one hundred feet below.

> 'The boast of heraldry, the pomp of pow'r,
> And all that beauty, all that wealth e'er gave,
> Awaits alike th' inevitable hour,

The paths of glory lead but to the grave.'

Epilogue

Two nights later Holmes and I found ourselves lighting a fire at 221B Baker Street. An emotional and physical reaction to the efforts and strains of the past weeks had overtaken me, although I suspect my friend was less affected than I. Both of us had spent many hours with the officialdom of Scotland Yard, and report after report had to be given and transcribed. Lestrade was to be given some sort of formal award for his part in the solution of the mysteries which had confounded us for the past several weeks, and for his heroism in saving Guri's life. The latter he richly deserved.

At the invitation of the Queen and Prince Edward, we had called at Buckingham Palace to receive the Royal thanks of a sorely tried Mother and her son. There was some talk about Holmes being included in the next Honors List, but he had gracefully declined, saying that his usefulness to all the people of England, great and small, would be diminished by his acceptance.

Because of an emergency involving one of my patients, I had been unable to accompany him when he called upon Ramo Samyi and Guri to report on his activities on their mutual behalf. Of course, he had wanted to hear from her all that had transpired during the nearly two months elapsing between her disappearance from the theatre, and her being found in the well in the ruins of the palace of Baron Jonathon.

Informally, he also met privately with Mr. Gladstone and Mr. Asquith, accounting to them his activities during the interim.

So it was, then, that we had not had opportunity for one of our usual instructive interlocutions, which over the years had become our habit, when my friend would explain for my benefit the conclusions he had reached and the actions he had taken as a result thereof.

Outside, the elements were reminding us that they, too, could confound and disrupt earlier promise. After a day of warm sunshine with the gentlest of westerly breezes, we were now treated to a series of showers and errant, strong gusts of wind. It was a night for a warm fireplace, a good cigar, a snifter of brandy and relaxed conversation.

"Holmes," I said, "there are several things about this entire conundrum that are still baffling to me."

"My dear Watson, we are long overdue for our usual post-adventure chat. I am entirely at your service."

"First of all," I responded, "if you knew from the very beginning - from the day of the explosion at the Tower - that the jewels had not been carried away by the Fenians, but were merely concealed in a false bottom of the display case, why, in the name of heaven, did you not say so at once? Why wait for these many weeks to make this revelation?"

"Watson, you must remember that there were two explosions at the Tower at virtually the same time. An attempt to rescue the Fenian prisoners, and to steal the jewels at the same time would be asking for detection. The risk of failure of either or both ventures would have increased in geometric progression because of the heightened attention and vigilance of the Beefeater guards and the immediately available security forces. The detonation at Wakefield Tower occurred first in point of time. This explosion and the disappearance of the Royal gems was an old magician's stratagem - a simple misdirection of attention while the principal objective is carried out - here, the escape of the Fenians. Do not forget, Watson, those prisoners had a date with the executioner's blade. For them time was running out at a rapid rate."

"But why did you not unmask the deception immediately?"

"Without question, both explosions were Fenian directed. It was obvious they wanted us to think they had the jewels. Why? Had we forthwith announced that we had not been duped, we could never have ascertained the reason they had only concealed the treasure rather than taken it. You see, Watson, I did not yet know their game. It was three days before the ransom note was delivered to the Queen. Only then did we learn of the kidnapping of Prince Edward. The price for his freedom was the financing of their continuing warfare against the Crown. Additionally, for them, it was a not-to-be-resisted chance to tweak the tail of the British lion."

"But, surely then would have been an opportune time to reveal the whereabouts of the jewels."

"No, Watson, it was still premature. Our major problem was the securing of the release of His Royal Highness. The treasure, symbol of the wealth and might of the country, was safe. No purpose would have been served by divulging their lodgment before we had Edward out of their hands. In fact, his safety would have been in even more jeopardy than it was, if we had found the jewels before we found him."

"How so, Holmes?"

"Because, my dear friend, if we had done so, the Fenians would have known that we had not been fooled, and might well have assumed we knew more about them, their activities and the kidnapping than we really did, including the location where the Prince was to be held."

I was silent for a time, digesting the information I had been given.

"Very well, my friend, tell me this: it is easy to understand the killing of the royal cabinetmaker and his hostage daughter. But why were the assistants of Robert-Houdin and Alexander Herrmann, namely Beverly Caldwell and Harold Dornn, also slaughtered in such a fashion?"

"Really, Watson, sometimes you disappoint me. That is one of the more easily discernible features of this case. The professional magician in his repertoire of illusions makes liberal use of devices which, because of their construction, cause items provided by the magician or his audience seem to inexplicably disappear. A performer would be lost without his sealed boxes or cabinets with false bottoms or sides into which the object vanishes without a trace to the utter mystification of the innocent participant. Beverly Caldwell and Harold Dornn were kidnapped, tortured, and then killed after they had revealed these secrets, including the details of traps, collapsible bases, springs, and all the other paraphernalia the artist employs for a public that truly wants to be fooled. Surely this must have been apparent to you."

"Of course. Of course, it is. Particularly now that you have explained it to me so clearly," I confessed rather sheepishly. "But that in no way explains Guri. She was abducted long after the fabricated cabinets had been in place at the Tower. She was taken the night before the bombing. And why wasn't she killed as were the others?"

"Ah, yes," my friend replied. "You were unable to attend me when I visited Guri and her husband yesterday. You have posed two questions in regard to that attractive young lady, and her account of that evening and the subsequent weeks provide answers to both.

"As to why she was kidnapped, there was only one plausible explanation. You are correct. She had nothing to do with the murders of her predecessors, the Crown Jewels, the kidnapping of the Prince - none of the things which have been central to this investigation. Except one. And that one provides the entire answer. During her performance at the Egyptian Hall, she observed the midget - our late nemesis - slip out of his harness. That incident escaped Samyi. She had to be silenced before she could inform her husband. Thus, when the cage which she occupied was covered with the red silken cloth, and she dropped though the trapdoor on the stage into the basement, even as the tiger was introduced to the cage, she was seized by our adversaries, chloroformed and hidden until they could safely return for her. You will call to mind the following afternoon when you and I made an extensive examination of the basement of the theatre, I was especially interested in that cage sized box with a sliding lid standing next to the wall, into which I thrust my head and shoulders for an appreciable length of time As I told you at the time, there was a readily detectable odor of chloroform inside that coffinlike receptacle. She was removed between the hours of midnight and dawn when no custodian was on duty.

"Now, as to your second question, why was she not killed? We must both admit she is a most attractive young lady. Enough to turn the head of any man, eh? All true, but why did Beverly Caldwell die? She too was alluring. Why was Guri's life spared? The answer, Watson, is as old as time itself, the love of a man for a maid. Midgets are human, too, my friend, and Baron Jonathon succumbed to the oldest emotion known to man. He was totally smitten with Guri and could not bring himself to order her execution.

"Why, then, did he seek to cause her death by drowning? His ardor had not been returned. His every effort had been repulsed. He knew we were on to him, and that we shortly would be laying siege to his fortress, relic that it was. Yet he could not bring himself to order the mutilation of her body - the crushing of her throat and the snapping of her lovely neck. He was reconciled to the fact that she must die, and in his twisted mind, it was better that her death be by drowning, away from his presence, her physical perfection unspoiled. He could not bear to remember her as misshapen by the indignities to which she would be subject at the hands of his giant."

"So, Cupid and his bow and arrow had a hand in this as well," I remarked. "How much of what you have just related to me had you deduced, Holmes?"

"Before I took my unceremonious departure from this world in the explosion of my carriage, I had concluded that we were dealing with an extremely small statured person and a giant, and that they both were going to somewhat grotesque lengths to keep the existence of the former a secret. It was my conclusion that Guri during her on-stage performance had seen the emergence of the midget from the giant's hump. Of that, I was fairly well satisfied. As I have said, Guri confirmed this yesterday.

"However, as to whether she would be found alive, I was not nearly so sanguine. But I felt that if she were resourceful enough, or if she recalled the story of Scheherazade, who kept herself alive for 1001 nights by telling the desert sheik a different story each night, then there was a better than even chance that she would survive. And, Watson, that is exactly what she did. She was the personal magician for Jonathon and his Ymir. The baron became enamored of her, to the end that when she had exhausted her inventory of illusions and magic, he was so smitten that the danger to her had largely passed."

"Amazing, absolutely amazing," I said. "I confess to you that when you disappeared, I gave up all hope of her ever being found alive. A most remarkable young lady. Tell me, Holmes, will these experiences of hers weigh so heavily upon her in the future so as to affect her life? Will she be all right?"

"Well, as you know, Watson, I am not any sort of physician to the human mind. But, from what I observed yesterday between Samyi and Guri, in spite of a mind-shattering existence of several weeks, I think his love and comfort will see her through in good order."

"That, indeed, is good news. When that poor girl was pulled from the well, I had grave doubts that she would ever again have a chance to live a normal life. But, to another subject, Holmes. In my own investigations following the bombing of your cab, I traced you to the university library. There I learned that, among other things, you had researched the MacNeill and O'Mahoney families as well as Charles Stewart Parnell. There was nothing about Jonathon Hyde."

"Watson, I must give you high marks for following in my footsteps to the athenaeum, and for learning the objects of my study. But, contrariwise, I must take some of your grade away. You failed to undertake a detailed examination of the materials. If you had, you, too, would have found that Jonathon was the son of Sir Alexander Hyde, the shipbuilder. Alexander Hyde's mother was a sister of the father of John O'Mahoney, one of the founders of the parent organization to the Fenians.

"What good did this information do me? We were then in a most delicate position. I knew the identity of the mastermind of the Fenians. I knew who had Guri. But I also knew the Fenians had Prince Edward, and we hadn't a clue as to the whereabouts of any of them. If I had given this information to Lestrade or any of his superiors at the Yard, then the whole bag would have been opened and I would have lost control of the situation.

"When we followed Jonathon and his tame giant to the warehouse, and when that structure was blown up, I knew he would go to ground, and then it became a simple matter of ascertaining his one safe, sure sanctuary. My books on heraldry gave me that answer. Is that explanation satisfactory, Watson?"

"Eminently so, my friend," I replied. "I know the hour is late, but you will oblige me greatly if you will tell me why, with all this information in your possession, you felt it necessary to have yourself killed off, so convincingly. Why?"

"My dear friend, I know it was a cruel thing to do to you. But the Fenians were on to me. As it was, they came preciously close to killing me. Their agents reported everything I did, wherever I went, and anybody with whom I had any contact whatsoever. I had to be eliminated. From their point of view, I constituted, the most formidable obstacle to their plans for terrorizing the government. As for me, I had to disappear so convincingly that they would assume I was dead, and could not, therefore, constitute any sort of threat. Had I simply vanished, Jonathon and his Ymir might never have come out into the open. There was no other way."

"You might at least have told me, or alternatively, your brother, Mycroft."

"My dear Watson, Mycroft did know. He was my coachman. When the irregular carried my notes that night to Lestrade and to my brother at the Diogenes Club, it was my signal to him that matters had progressed to the point where our prearranged plan must be put into effect immediately, and that plan was that I should appear to die in order that my life be spared to continue the investigation.

"As you have occasion to know, Watson, that is not the first time my brother has been employed in a similar capacity. You, yourself, enjoyed his services when we were trying to slip out of London to elude Professor Moriarity. Our adventure there ended at Reichenbach Falls.

"But, my loyal and trusted friend, to tell you of all of this and of my plans to die in an explosion in a hansom cab, was totally impossible. In spite of the grief it was certain to cause, you were the last person in whom I could confide. To save your own life, the less you knew the better, because your too, Watson, were under constant surveillance. Were you in possession of the knowledge I had, or had you even suspected it, I would have been mourning you."

"But, Holmes, even if I accept your premise on that subject, in the name of heaven, how did you escape that explosion? I saw it, and I identified some of your clothing and even your remains at the Yard at the time of the Inquiry the following day."

"Illusions, Watson, nothing but illusions. Oh, the cap, pipe and shoe were real enough. It was intended that they should burn. The bones and charred flesh were from a slaughterhouse. All were stage props to heighten the illusion.

"But the explosion is a different matter entirely. Several years ago, in anticipation of its future necessity, Mycroft and I arranged to have a standard hansom cap specially modified and equipped with steel plating in a box around the driver. It was our reasoning that when its use became essential, it would be a simple matter for the passenger to slip through a sliding door in the plate to join the driver, where both would be protected from whatever lethal device should be thrown or placed into the cab. And it worked, Watson, it worked! As you know, Mycroft's position in Whitehall permits him access to the various departments which comprise the English government. I think it only fair to tell you that his report on the success of our armor plate is already on file in the War Office. I predict that someday some military or naval tactician will appreciate its promise and will utilize its potential for our Army or Navy."

"There was another curious aspect to the departure of your carriage, however, Holmes," I responded. "The rear wheels were blown off, and I followed the tracks of the front wheels, and the dragging undercarriage for some distance. But then something strange happened. The marks of the dragging undercarriage disappeared, and while the hoof marks of the horses and the prints of the front wheels continued onward, a third wheel mark seemed to appear positioned nearly midway between the other two."

"Another aspect of the reconstruction of the hansom, Watson. When the armor was installed, we also provided for a recessed third wheel which could be lowered by hand pumping from the seat of the cab. This, of course, was to remove the drag and friction of the back of the cab as it was pulled along a pavement, and to make the conveyance more stable. Naturally, when the third wheel makes contact with the ground, speed is increased, the observer is mystified, and escape is facilitated."

"What did you do then?"

"I continued my investigations for a time, utilizing some of my more appropriate disguises. When I had decided upon the proper method of unmasking our quarry, I went to the Continent for a short time, and, under the tutelage of my friend, M. Houdin, mastered the Indian rope trick which you saw. I knew that Baron Jonathon would not be able to resist attending a new show of magic. He is even more of an enthusiast than I. As I said earlier, this is what saved Guri's life. The rest you know."

One other question was burning to be asked. "I say, Holmes, would you bend a rule of yours and tell me how that Indian rope illusion is accomplished?"

Holmes regarded me gravely. "My dear friend, as much as I am in your debt for the weeks when you thought me dead, this

I cannot do. I have sworn a solemn oath that that secret shall not pass my lips." Then, with a twinkle in his eye, he continued, "However, I can give you this much: When one has mastered the principle of levitation, the rest is quite simple. You know, Watson, there are but a handful of artists in the world who can perform that illusion, and that number was reduced by one with the death of Jonathon Hyde."

"Holmes, what are you saying?"

"My good friend, Jonathon was the bomber. I thought that was apparent. Just after the explosion, you will recall, Lestrade chased what he thought to be a young boy. Lestrade was in error. It was Jonathon, and he made his escape on the street in exactly the same way that I climbed the rope and disappeared on the stage."

"But why did our diminutive adversary expose himself to that risk? Any number of Fenians would have obeyed his command instantly. Why Jonathon himself?"

"Two reasons, Watson. An extremely short statured man needs to feel just as masculine as his large neighbor, and he must constantly reassure himself on that subject. The Emperor Napoleon is an example. In personally undertaking the bombing, Jonathon was asserting his equality with the strongest and most courageous soldier in the Fenian army. Secondly, by this time, my death had become a private obsession with him, and he, alone, was going to savor the experience."

"Just before you departed our lodgings here on the night you disappeared, you told me that because of the information you possessed, your life was in danger. What led you to that conclusion?"

"There were several bits and pieces of knowledge which I had accumulated, Watson, which forced me to make that deduction. Earlier this evening I recounted for you my research at the library which revealed the relationship between the O'Mahoney and Hyde families. I already knew we were dealing with two people - a midget and a giant - and that the former was the instigating genius behind the terror which the latter was permitted to employ. I would not have had a chance in an encounter with Ymir. Of course, I also knew that the main purpose of the bombing at the Tower was to enable the Fenians to escape.

"They were getting too close to me, Watson. And when from the window I observed what you took to be a young lad in surveillance of our flat here, I knew that they had determined to carry out their plan of assassination that night, taking advantage of the filthy weather. Thus, it was my decision to seize the initiative and disappear, leaving them with the conviction that their plot had been successful."

We were silent for quite a period of time. For my part, I was recalling the events which led up to the flight of my friend, the weeks without him filled with sorrow, but, nevertheless, pursuing the investigations on my own, his miraculous reappearance from what I had thought to be his grave, and the activities in which we together had engaged to bring this incredible sequence of happenings to a successful conclusion.

The embers in the fireplace had cooled, and the room was noticeably more chilly. Outside, the elements still visited us with showers, and occasionally a window rattled in a sudden burst of wind.

From his chair on the right of the fireplace, Holmes at last rose to his feet.

"Watson, I, for one, am fatigued, and in need of rest. If you wish, we can continue this discussion another day." He crossed behind me on the way to his bedroom. He paused at its door, and then, with just the faintest sound of mirth in his voice, he added a comment, which, quite literally, paralyzed my muscular and pulmonary systems as thoroughly as a sudden blow to the solar plexus.

"By the way, old friend, and forgive me for an irresistibly, inelegant insolence – I'll never forgive you, Watson, for your 'pendulously, ponderous pachyderm' some evening when we both are so inclined, you will have to favor me with an account of your investigations at 55 Eaton Terrace."

A peal of uncharacteristic Holmesian laughter accompanied the closing of his bedroom door.